ORTHO'S All About

Successful Perennial Gardening

Written by Janet Macunovich

Meredith® Books
Des Moines, Iowa

Ortho® Books
An imprint of Meredith® Books

All About Successful Perennial Gardening
Editor: Marilyn Rogers
Writer: Janet Macunovich
Contributing Editor: Catherine Hamrick
Senior Associate Design Director: Tom Wegner
Assistant Editor: Harijs Priekulis
Copy Chief: Terri Fredrickson
Managers, Book Production: Pam Kvitne,
    Marjorie J. Schenkelberg
Contributing Copy Editor: Barbara Feller-Roth
Contributing Proofreaders: Mary Duerson, Alison M.
    Glascock, Sandra Neff, Barbara Stokes
Contributing Map Illustrator: Jana Fothergill
Indexer: Ellen Davenport
Electronic Production Coordinator: Paula Forest
Editorial and Design Assistants: Kathleen Stevens,
    Karen Schirm

**Additional Editorial Contributions from
Art Rep Services**
Director: Chip Nadeau
Designers: lk Design
Illustrator: Dave Brandon

Meredith® Books
Editor in Chief: James D. Blume
Design Director: Matt Strelecki
Managing Editor: Gregory H. Kayko
Executive Editor, Gardening and Home Improvement:
    Benjamin W. Allen

Director, Sales, Special Markets: Rita McMullen
Director, Sales, Premiums: Michael A. Peterson
Director, Sales, Retail: Tom Wierzbicki
Director, Book Marketing: Brad Elmitt
Director, Operations: George A. Susral
Director, Production: Douglas M. Johnston

Meredith Publishing Group
President, Publishing Group: Stephen M. Lacy

Meredith Corporation
Chairman and Chief Executive Officer: William T. Kerr
Chairman of the Executive Committee: E.T. Meredith III

Thanks to
Janet Anderson, Rosemary A. Kautzky, Mary Irene Swartz

Photographers
    (Photographers credited may retain copyright ©
    to the listed photographs.)
L = Left, R = Right, C = Center, B = Bottom, T = Top
Williams Adams: 70BL, 78T; **R. Adkins:** 55TCL; **Gay
Bumgarner/Positive Image:** 4BL, 36T, 44T, 64B, 67BR; **David
Cavagnaro:** 37TL, 54B, 55TCR, 69T, 72T, 82TL, 82B, 90T, 106T;
A. Crozier: 47TC; **R. Todd Davis:** 65BL, 87BR, 88B, 89B;
Richard Day: 4BC; **Alan and Linda Detrick/gardenIMAGE:** 59B;
Catriona Tudor Erler: 4T, 35BR, 63BR, 68B, 71T, 90B, 97TR,
105T; **Derek Fell:** 3, 67TC, 68T, 83TR; **Susan M. Glascock:** 66C,
66B; **John Glover:** 4BR, 72B, 78BC, 99BL, 99BR; **David
Goldberg:** 20B, 21; **Anne Gordon:** 102B; **Saxon Holt:** 59C, 67BL,
95B, 100T, 106BC; **Bill Johnson:** 48T, 63T, 74T, 98TL, 101B,
103T; **Rosemary A. Kautzky:** 45BL, 58BR, 65, 73T, 79BL, 81T,
85BL, 89T, 103B; **Donna & Tom Krischan:** 5, 54T, 61B, 80B,
81BR, 92T, 104B; **Michael Landis:** 6, 31R1, 31R2, 31R4, 31R5,
31R6, 31B, 34; **Andrew Lawson:** 63BC, 63BL, 70T, 80T, 81BL,
83BL, 86T, 91T, 93B, 94B, 101T, 107B; **Scott Leonhart/Positive
Images:** 45BR; **Janet Loughrey:** 57, 77TR, 79TC, 86C, 87T;
Bryan McCay: 20T; **Michael McKinley:** 24, 43T; **Steven Nikkila:**
7, 11, 12, 13, 14, 15, 16, 17TR, 17B, 18, 19, 26, 27, 29, 31TL,
35BL, 36BL, 36BR, 37BC, 40, 42, 43BL, 43BR, 44B, 52, 58T, 60T,
61T, 62T, 65BCR, 67TL, 73BL, 73BR, 75, 76BR, 77TL, 78BR,
79TL, 79TR, 83BR, 85TL, 85TR, 87BL, 88T, 92B, 95T, 97B,
99BC, 100B, 107T; **Jerry Pavia:** 8, 37TC, 37TR, 60B, 62B, 69BR,
86B, 91B, 98TC; **Ben Phillips/Positive Images:** 71B, 82TR, 93TC,
97TL, 98TR; **C.C. Powell:** 51B; **Marilyn Rogers:** 45T; **Richard
Shiell:** 76BL, 79BC, 99T; **Lark Smotherman:** 10T, 22C2, 22C3,
22B, 31R3; **Albert Squillace/Positive Images:** 94T; **Joseph G.
Strauch, Jr.:** 37BR, 58BL, 65BLC, 69BL, 93TL, 96B, 102T, 104T,
106BR; **Steve Struse:** 17TL; **Studio Central:** 10B, 22T, 22C1,
22C4; **L. Swezey:** 47B; **Peter Symcox/gardenIMAGE:** 79BL, 84T;
Michael S. Thompson: 55BCR, 65BR, 66T, 74B, 76TL, 84B,
85BR, 96T, 98B, 105B; **Connie Toops:** 77B, 88C, 93TR;
University of California: 46BR; **Deidra Walpole:** 58BC; **Kay
Wheeler:** 76TR, 79BR; **Justyn Willsmore:** 37BL, 59T, 64T, 67TR,
70BR, 82TC, 83TL, 106BL

Cover photo: Derek Fell

All of us at Ortho® Books are dedicated to providing you
with the information and ideas you need to enhance your
home and garden. We welcome your comments and
suggestions about this book. Write to us at:
    Meredith Corporation
    Ortho Gardening Books
    1716 Locust St.
    Des Moines, IA 50309–3023

If you would like to purchase any of our gardening, home
improvement, cooking, crafts, or home decorating and
design books, check wherever quality books are sold. Or visit
us at: meredithbooks.com

If you would like more information on other Ortho
products, call 800-225-2883 or visit us at: www.ortho.com

Note to the Readers: Due to differing conditions, tools,
and individual skills, Meredith Corporation assumes no
responsibility for any damages, injuries suffered, or losses
incurred as a result of following the information published
in this book. Before beginning any project, review the
instructions carefully, and if any doubts or questions remain,
consult local experts or authorities. Always read and observe
all of the safety precautions provided by manufacturers of
any tools, equipment, or supplies, and follow all accepted
safety procedures.

Perennials shine in the spring. Even before most annual beds are planted, columbine and woodland phlox light up the garden.

Songbirds, such as this American goldfinch, are drawn to the ripening seeds of many perennials in the daisy family, including purple coneflower.

Frost may end annual displays but mark the height of the fall perennial season (asters, goldenrod, maiden grass and mums in fall).

There are no dull moments in a perennial garden. Spring bloomers bow out as the summer show introduces a whole new lineup of interesting flower colors and forms.

PERENNIALS THE MOST VERSATILE PLANTS

Perennial gardening means more than growing flowers that come back year after year. It's an adventure! You'll discover how versatile these plants can be—how they will enrich your garden with more than beautiful blooms.

Plants you meet as flat pictures on a page or pot tag will grow to reveal intriguing dimensions. You'll enjoy sharing their distinctive colors and shapes. Neighbors will admire how perennial beds beautify your surroundings. And friends will like receiving gorgeous bouquets.

You'll also have the pleasure of pursuing your hobby through more than one season. Months before marigolds and impatiens start to color others' yards, Bethlehem sage, Lenten rose, and catmint will have put on a show in the perennial garden. Long after annuals fade in late summer heat, perennial asters, sedums, and Japanese anemones make their debut. The coral bells you select for sprays of red flowers will end up pleasing you with their durable winter presence. You can extend the season even further with arrangements of seedpods and dried foliage that dress a perennial bed right through winter.

Perennials can be a gift you pass on to another generation. Just think—the lush peony that captures your imagination in spring will live on to become a family heirloom.

Almost all perennials live at least three years. But some, such as peonies, can anchor a garden for decades. Yet perennials are not as permanent as a shrub or as intimidating to place as a tree. Trees and shrubs are to a garden what walls and roof are to a home. Perennials are the furnishings—dependable but changeable.

Increasingly, gardeners are moving perennials out of traditional beds and into larger roles in the landscape as foundation plants, ground covers, and minishrubs. Instead of pruning shrubs to keep them lower than a window ledge or narrow enough to hedge the sidewalk, planting perennials such as Russian sage, astilbe, or fringecups provides as much interest and greenery—without the overbearing size. You'll discover geranium or lady's mantle to be plants that can cover ground and suppress weeds while putting on a floral display. If your landscape requires a fast hedge, consider ornamental grasses, which mature quicker and are easier to maintain than shrubs.

Perennials bring personal pleasure as well. Make your garden a haven of learning experiences for the family. Your plants will attract wildlife, such as songbirds drawn to black-eyed Susan seeds or butterflies to Joe-Pye weed blossoms. Learn and tell your children the lore of plants, such as the stories linked to bleeding heart and obedient plant.

Ultimately, perennial gardening is a rewarding hobby that transforms your yard into a setting where fun, satisfaction, and beauty prevail, even as it relieves stress. This book will help you reap the most from your efforts by showing how to prepare soil for optimum growth, and how to select and care for plants suited to your site and budget. The extensive plant gallery will enhance the experience. Here's your chance to learn time-honored and cutting-edge techniques that will make your perennial garden a showplace!

Color, fragrance, and variety attract children to perennial gardens. They often stay to join the gardener in two common perennial pastimes— having fun and learning new skills.

GREAT GROUNDWORK MAKES A GREAT GARDEN

When you improve the soil before planting you make a smart investment. It yields a high return in prettier, healthier, sturdier, lower-care perennials.

Next year's performance is built into this year's perennial roots. Thus success starts with making the soil around the roots the best it can be.

Perennials grow the fastest, are the sturdiest and healthiest, and bloom the brightest in loose, well-drained, weed-free, fertile loam with a pH of about 6.5. Before planting, figure out which of these characteristics your soil lacks, then fix it.

It's best to work the soil in fall so it can settle over winter and be ready for spring planting. But whatever time of year you're able to do the work, make sure the soil is friable. Squeeze a handful of soil, then open your hand. The soil should not ooze water but readily crumble when poked.

LOOSE SOIL

Loose soil has lots of pore space for air and water to move through. Think of it this way: In a 2-quart pot of soil, air and water should take up the equivalent of 1 quart of space. In loose soil, perennial roots spread wide and fast. The plants are steadier in wind and unlikely to topple over as they reach full height. With their wider spread, the roots have more resources from which to draw water and nutrients.

Many soils need loosening because they're dense or compacted from foot traffic, grading, or seasonal flooding. As an example, just eight passes with a bulldozer during construction or relandscaping work reduces air and water space in a soil that had the ideal 50 percent to only 5 to 10 percent. Kids' play can be nearly as hard on the soil.

Perennials grow best in beds with loose soil 18 inches deep, but you need dig only as deep as necessary to loosen the compacted layer. Sometimes only the top few inches of soil may be dense, but it's also common to find a compacted layer about 9 inches below the surface under relatively loose soil. This deeper compaction may exist because your proposed

SINGLE-DIGGING

DOUBLE-DIGGING

Use a spade or spading fork to loosen the top 8 to 10 inches if the soil is an acceptable loam, drainage is good, and no compacted layer exists within the top 18 inches. Loosen the soil by inserting the fork to its full depth, then pulling back on the handle to lever the tines. You can compost any sod stripped from the area.

Dig a 9-inch-deep trench across the bed, stockpiling soil on a tarp. With a fork, loosen the trench bottom to 9 inches deep; top with compost. Dig a second trench, tossing the soil into the first. Loosen, add compost, and continue to the end of the bed. Fill the last trench with the set-aside soil. Rake to level the soil; soil will settle but be higher than before. Avoid standing in the trenches.

garden was farmland or a vegetable garden repeatedly tilled to that depth.

Soil is loose if you can easily dig in it. If you must soak the soil before digging or need to use a pickax to make a hole, it needs loosening. You can loosen soil by hand or with a tiller.

BY HAND: Use a spade or spading fork (the fork's tines better penetrate dense soil) to cut, lift, or reset soil. Manual loosening works best in small areas; in weedy areas where each square foot of soil must be inspected and cleared of weed roots; in existing beds between established plants and tree roots; and in soil that must be loosened deeper than the tiller's 9- to 10-inch reach.

Single-dig to loosen well-drained loam. Double-dig to break up hardpan (a layer of soil densely packed by machinery or traffic, preventing the free flow of water and air), or to loosen soil 18 inches deep, if necessary. (See the illustrations at left.)

TILLING: As rototillers slice, lift, cut, and drop soil in chunks, they increase the amount of air between soil clods.

Tilling is practical only in new, large gardens free of tree and perennial weed roots. Small areas offer no room to maneuver. Tree roots deflect tines, and perennial weed roots tend to multiply when chopped.

Avoid overtilling and working in wet soil. Soil cut too many times by a tiller or shovel becomes structureless, like sifted flour. Till only enough to turn, not pulverize. Shoveling or tilling wet soil can churn it into a concretelike slurry. Both conditions make it hard for air and water to move through the soil.

Repeated tilling can cause hardpan. Check every few seasons at the 8- to 9-inch depth to see if one is developing.

Turning or tilling soil is a good time to add materials to help prevent future compaction. Use porous substances that don't crush easily and have relatively large particles, such as coarse builder's sand, composted pine bark, or commercial additives, such as Perlite, Turface, or Profile. Before turning or tilling, spread a 2- to 3-inch layer of the material over the

area. Then mix it into the entire depth that needs loosening.

Materials that act like magnets to soil particles, such as compost, composted pine bark, and gypsum (calcium sulfate) are even better additives. Grains of clay and sand gradually attach themselves to the additives, so the soil becomes rounded crumbs rather than densely packed layers. Gypsum is most effective in saline soils.

Tillers are useful for loosening topsoil or mixing in amendments from 2 to 10 inches deep. Caution: Till only to mix or loosen—not pulverize—to avoid destroying soil structure. Avoid tilling wet soil; that will destroy soil structure. Small-statured gardeners find rear-tine, self-propelled tillers easier to operate.

In large areas, rent the equipment used to install irrigation lines. It knifes the soil to cut slits 2 feet apart and as deep as the blades reach. Under trees, auger 18-inch-deep holes 2 feet apart.

Sheet composting gradually loosens soil between established plants and around tree roots. Spread organic materials in a 2- to 3-inch layer over the soil. Keep moist. Grubs, soil bacteria, fungi, and earthworms mix the materials into the soil for you. To speed up the process, poke holes into the soil with a fork before spreading the materials.

PROTECT YOUR FEET

Make soil preparation easier and protect your feet by wearing boots whenever you dig. Choose hard-soled boots that support your ankle and have a low but definite heel so you can rest your foot securely on the tread of the shovel.

GREAT GROUNDWORK MAKES A GREAT GARDEN
continued

DRAINAGE FOR HEALTHY PLANTS

Drainage describes how water and oxygen move through the soil. Water flows through soil pores, drawing air behind it. Well-drained soil is the ideal combination of water and oxygen. It feels like a moist sponge.

Many plant failures are linked to drainage, and it can be difficult to recognize the connection. Both excessively wet and dry soil inhibits root growth. In wet soil, plants grow poorly, need staking, die back, wilt, and come under attack from insects and diseases. Even though hardy, such plants may die in winter.

Poorly drained soil holds too much water, is soggy, and may smell sour. Excessively drained soil, such as sand, generally does not store water. Keeping it moist is a challenge.

Drainage is easy to test and well worth the effort—do it before planting to prevent costly problems in the future. (See the boxes below and on page 9.)

This bed needed to be raised for drainage. Building up the bed up at its sides maximizes the area. You could simply hill up the soil. But that improves drainage only at the center of the hill, not at the sides, which are barely above the original grade. Raising a bed even higher would let you work without bending.

PREVENT WEEDS

Weeds are unsightly and compete with perennials for water, light, and nutrients. Any weeds left in a bed after preparing the soil will be back. Take steps to eradicate or block them. Persistent weeds, such as dandelions and perennial grasses especially, can return from overlooked root remnants and tangle with your perennials. Then you'll be forced to uproot the perennial to remove the weed.

Before tilling under or removing sod or existing plants for the new bed, identify what else is growing there; then you can take the right steps to prevent weeds.

Turfgrasses are relatively shallow rooted and easy to kill. Till them under, mulch heavily, and wait two to three weeks for remnants to resprout. Then weed out these sprouts or treat them with a nonselective, nonresidual herbicide, such as glyphosate (Roundup) or glufosinate-ammonium. Alternatively, physically remove the lawn by digging it out with a spade.

TESTING DRAINAGE

How well do water and air move through your soil? Don't be misled by the type of soil. Even clay can drain well, and sand can drain poorly. To check drainage, first you have to dig an 18-inch-deep test hole. Fill the hole with water and let it drain. This thoroughly wets the soil along the sides of the hole. Fill the hole again.

Next, record the inches of water left in the hole after one day. This information tells you whether you need to raise the bed to improve drainage. For example, if 9 inches of water remain after one day, raising the bed 9 inches is advisable. Finally, note the total time required for the hole to drain.

■ If the soil is excessively well drained, the hole empties in less than 3½ hours.
■ If the soil is well drained, the hole empties in 3½ to 24 hours.
■ If the soil is moderately well drained, the hole empties in 24 to 72 hours.
■ If the soil is poorly drained, the hole empties in 3½ to 7 days.
■ If the soil is very poorly drained, the hole empties after 7 days.

Standard lawn edging, which extends 4 to 5 inches into the ground and comes in 20-foot strips or rolls, usually restrains the roots of lawn grass but does not stop deeper-running species such as quackgrass. Carpet runner, protective plastic sold in 27-inch-wide rolls, can be used as a deeper barrier. Slice it lengthwise to make strips as wide as the rooting depth of nearby weeds (for example, three 9-inch-wide or four 6½-inch-wide strips).

TOUGHER WEEDS

Perennial weeds, such as thistle, dandelions, bermudagrass, kikuyugrass, quackgrass, and bindweed, are a different case. They require deep, careful digging to remove all running roots. Avoid tilling live perennial weeds. They will reemerge and slow establishment of the ornamentals.

One control method is to loosen the soil, then dig up the weeds or spray an herbicide. Wait 60 days to plant the garden, digging or killing any sprouts that pop up. This method works only during the growing season.

Another strategy involves treating the area with herbicide, waiting for top growth to die, mowing the dead vegetation short, and reapplying weed killer as needed over a 60-day period. Then till or turn the area to break up the dead roots. Be aware, tilling brings up seeds of annual weeds.

Use an herbicide absorbed through the plant's leaves, such as glyphosate or 2-4D; check the label to see if the herbicide has residual activity. Some root-absorbed herbicides remain in the soil and stunt or damage new perennials for some time.

ANNUAL WEEDS

Where annual weeds, such as crabgrass and purslane, dominate, turn the soil, or apply herbicide. Later, till in the dead residue. Mulch or mix a preemergent weed killer, such as trifluralin (Treflan), into the top inch of soil to prevent reinfestations.

KEEP OUT NEW WEEDS

After cleaning up the bed, the last step is to note nearby sources of weeds and prevent them from reinvading. If weedy neighbors spread by below-ground runners, install a vertical root barrier around the bed. To bar weeds that creep on the surface (for example, ground ivy), periodically remove or kill them at the garden edge. Mowing discourages weeds that spread by seed, such as many annuals and some perennials (violets and dandelions).

WHAT TO DO WITH THE RESULTS OF THE DRAINAGE TEST

If your soil is...	Then you should...
Excessively well drained	Mix a 2- to 3-inch layer of moisture-retentive amendments (compost or clay soil) into the bed. Mulch with materials that break down within a year. Grow drought-tolerant plants. Check soil moisture frequently; water carefully, using drip irrigation systems or soaker hoses.
Well drained	Do nothing special. Grow all types of plants.
Moderately well drained	Grow species suited to moist, well-drained soil. Or raise the bed 1 inch for every inch of water left in the test hole after one day.
Poorly drained	Install drain tile, raise the bed 1 inch for every inch of water left in the test hole after one day, or grow only species suited to moist soil and imperfect drainage.
Very poorly drained	Install drain tile. Or raise the bed 1 inch for every inch of water left in the test hole after one day. Or grow only species suited to wet soil. Water carefully, delaying irrigation until the top few inches of soil have been dry for as many days as the test hole held water.

GREAT GROUNDWORK MAKES A GREAT GARDEN
continued

Amendments for fertility and structure:

Greensand, a rock powder, provides potassium and some phosphorus.

Cottonseed meal supplies nitrogen and some phosphorus and potassium.

Steamed bonemeal supplies phosphorus and a small amount of nitrogen.

Dried poultry manure provides nitrogen, phosphorus, and potassium.

Fertility is a measure of the type and amount of nutrients that plants can obtain from soil. The main source of nutrients is mineral matter—the sand, silt, and clay that make up a soil. Water clinging to soil particles gradually breaks down the minerals and becomes nutrient-rich. The plants absorb and use this water. Because of its tiny particles and porous structure, clay is more fertile than sand.

Another source of nutrients is humus—decomposing organic matter that darkens the soil.

A rough gauge of fertility can be gained from looking at the grass and weeds growing in the future garden spot and the soil's color. If the bed is dark clay that supported lush growth in the recent past, treat it as a naturally fertile soil that doesn't need heavy or special fertilization. Add a soil test to your list of tasks to do eventually. But if the soil is sandy and light in color, and plants did not grow well, mix in ½ pound of 10-10-10 fertilizer, then make it a priority to get the soil tested by a lab before the growing season is too far gone.

No matter the soil type, you can mix in up to ½ pound of 10-10-10 fertilizer or ¼ pound of 20-20-20 per 100 square feet of bed. This supplies the most important nutrients (nitrogen, phosphorus, and potassium) in equal amounts during the first season. Rake it lightly into the top few inches of the soil. The granules will dissolve and spread down.

IMPROVE SOIL STRUCTURE

Any soil can be made loose, well-drained, and weed free. However, for the best combination of these traits, plus fertility and moisture retention, the ideal is loam.

Loam is a mix of sand, silt, and clay. That is, loam has enough tiny clay particles (20 percent) to be fertile, enough large sand particles (40 percent) to drain quickly and warm up early in spring, and enough medium-sized silt particles (40 percent) to unite the clay and sand in loose, round crumbs. When topsoil is needed to build up existing soil, it's best to bring in a loam.

Your soil may have an excess of one particle type, which can cause problems. For example, excess clay makes for a sticky soil that clumps, preventing water and nutrients from passing through. Overly sandy soil is unable to retain moisture or nutrients. In such situations, gardeners often focus on changing the texture of the soil (relative amounts of sand, silt, and clay). But improving the structure (the way individual soil particles bind together) is a better way to improve plant growth and is sometimes easier to change than texture.

Well-structured soil breaks apart into small granules. It holds water, air, and nutrients better than poorly structured soil, which collapses into disconnected grains when wet.

To improve soil structure, add organic matter at every opportunity. Microorganisms feed on the organic matter and produce a "glue" that coats mineral particles and causes them to hold together in moisture-, air-, and nutrient-retaining crumbs.

Till or turn organic matter into the soil as you prepare the bed or add it by sheet composting. Aim for a 2- to 3-inch layer of moistened peat or compost, or a 3- to 4-inch layer of tree leaves. Keep the organic matter content high by using an organic mulch and natural forms of fertilizers such as manure.

MAINTAINING GOOD SOIL

Routinely loosen soil by cultivating regularly with a hoe, minitiller, or fork. This is especially important in soils with a high percentage of silt because these tend to "cap"—the surface layer becomes dense and nearly impervious to air and water.

To test structure, put a handful of soil in a sieve. Gently lower the sieve into a bowl of water, then lift it out and look for soil particles left in the water. The better the soil structure, the less there will be. In the garden, fewer nutrients will leach away when water passes through the soil.

ACID, NEUTRAL, AND ALKALINE SOIL—PERENNIALS FOR EVERY pH

Most perennials grow well if the soil pH is between 6 and 7, but some prefer more acid, others more alkaline conditions. Here are representatives of the various groups:

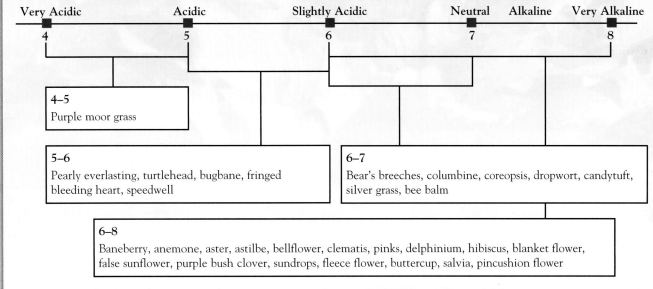

Very Acidic — Acidic — Slightly Acidic — Neutral — Alkaline — Very Alkaline
4   5   6   7   8

4–5
Purple moor grass

5–6
Pearly everlasting, turtlehead, bugbane, fringed bleeding heart, speedwell

6–7
Bear's breeches, columbine, coreopsis, dropwort, candytuft, silver grass, bee balm

6–8
Baneberry, anemone, aster, astilbe, bellflower, clematis, pinks, delphinium, hibiscus, blanket flower, false sunflower, purple bush clover, sundrops, fleece flower, buttercup, salvia, pincushion flower

Also spread a 1- to 3-inch blanket of organic matter on the soil surface as a mulch to encourage worms and soil microorganisms. Add amendments (the same you used when preparing the bed) in small amounts every time you rearrange, add, or divide plants in the bed.

SOIL TEXTURE

Total depth: 3"
Clay: ½" or more, making it 16% of total. Clay settles in several days to a week.
Silt: 1", 33% of total. Silt settles in 10 to 180 minutes.
Sand: 1½", 33% of total. Sand settles in 10 minutes.
Conclusion: Sandy soil

Put 1 cup of soil and 1 tablespoon of dishwasher detergent in a quart jar. Fill jar with water; cap and shake. Particles settle in this order: sand, then silt, organic matter, and clay. The depth of each layer gives clues as to soil type. Measure the total depth of the soil that settles out; then measure each layer. Divide layer depths by total depth.
■ Loam: 40% sand, 40% silt, 20% clay.
■ Sandy soil: more than 50% sand. May dry out and nutrients leach rapidly. Monitor watering; use degradable mulch; apply fertilizer frequently, lightly.
■ Clay soil: more than 25% clay. Tends to pack down. Add organic matter; use degradable mulch; avoid walking on bed.
■ Silt soil: more than 40% silt. Tends to pack down, excluding air and causing water to bead up and run off. Add organic matter; use degradable mulch; avoid walking on bed.

CHANGING SOIL pH

The ideal pH for most perennials is between 6.5 and 5.5 (mildly acid to acid). To measure soil pH, have the soil tested through the county extension office or obtain a test kit from a garden center. Lower pH with sulfur (ground soil sulfur, iron sulfate, or flowers of sulfur); raise it with lime (agricultural or dolomitic limestone). Thoroughly mix these materials into the top 6 to 8 inches of soil in the fall before planting. The change will last a season or longer. Retest soil before adding sulfur or lime again.

If Soil Is...	Add...per 100 square feet
Clay	
To lower pH 1 point	2 pounds of soil sulfur or 7½ pounds of iron sulfate
To raise pH 1 point	10½ pounds of limestone
Sandy	
To lower pH 1 point	1 pound of soil sulfur or 3 pounds of iron sulfate
To raise pH 1 point	2¾ pounds of limestone
Loam	
To lower pH by 1 point	1½ pounds of soil sulfur or 5 pounds of iron sulfate
To raise pH 1 point	7½ pounds of limestone

CAREFUL SELECTION ENSURES SUCCESS—BEAUTIFULLY

Perennials come in many sizes. Here's an assortment: cell pack (A); 3-inch pot (B); 2-quart pot (C); 6-inch pot (D); 8-inch or 1-gallon pot (E); 5-gallon tub (F). Rooted cutting (G); division (H); field-grown clump (I).

You've worked hard to lay the groundwork. Now you're ready for the fun—choosing perennials that will enhance your surroundings with stunning flowers and foliage.

Before you head for a garden center or leaf through catalogs, do a little more homework. Know the cold-hardiness for your region, indicated by the USDA map in the back of the book. Also review the growing conditions in your yard—areas may vary. Is the soil in the beds well- or poorly drained? Fertile or lean? Does it steadily retain moisture or dry out between waterings? Will your perennials get full sun or part shade? Are some spots windier than others?

Take notes to have handy while mulling over plant choices and shopping. This information is vital to the future well-being of your garden. When matched to the site, your perennials will be full, bloom readily, and stand a better chance of fending off insects and disease. Then peruse the "Plant Gallery" starting on page 56 to find the plants that will please you and will happily— and healthfully—grow in your yard.

Finally, think about where you'll find plants. The Yellow Pages can direct you to local garden centers. Mail-order sources can be reached by phone or the Internet. Local newspapers' gardening sections may announce perennial plant swaps in your area. Here's an overview of each source and their pros and cons.

GARDEN CENTERS

Buying at garden centers lets you carry out your purchases and plant them right away. Experts there can help you fine-tune your shopping list and answer questions about plants in stock, which you may not have researched. The perennials may carry a guarantee, and the garden center's location may make replacement convenient.

In general, plants at garden centers are available in 4-inch pots or gallon containers. Some offer even smaller or larger sizes.

Garden centers tend to stock only several hundred of the tens of thousands of existing perennial species and varieties. Relying solely on a local garden center means you may need

Space perennials so they won't be crowded during the two- to four-year establishment phase. These perennials were just planted.

In year two, fast-growing species nearly fill their spaces. Some grow more slowly—often these are longer-lived species.

By year three, some fast-growing plants already need dividing. Slower species can grow for many years without division.

to make substitutions for the original choices on your list.

MAIL ORDER

Mail order lets you shop without pulling out of the driveway. But the real enticement is being able to track down specific varieties not available at local garden centers, as well as having a choice of size and price.

To get started, consult references, such as *Gardening by Mail* by Barbara J. Barton and *The Andersen Horticultural Library's Source List of Plants & Seeds*. Or, with a couple of keystrokes, put the Internet to work. Enter a specific plant name in a search engine. You'll turn up dozens of online catalogs offering that plant.

Remember, with mail-order sources, you won't be able to inspect plants close up. A catalog might indicate plant size, but quality may be unknown. It's wise to limit your first order until you're acquainted with the quality and size of plants sent by a particular retailer.

Mail-order selections usually arrive potted or bare-root (dormant, with roots protected in a moist medium). It's also possible to find perennials as first year seedlings packed in plastic cells, typically six to a pack. Perennials in six packs cost much less than container-grown plants. If you buy plants this small, however, you may have to wait an extra year for a strong garden display. Try to plant your order as soon as possible. If you must wait a few days, keep plants moist and cool. Do not store them longer than a week.

GROWING PLANTS FROM SEED

Starting plants from seed appeals to many people. Seeds cost less than plants, and it's fascinating to watch the plants develop. However, do think about expenses beyond seed packets, including seed-starting potting medium, containers, and grow-lights and the electricity to run them. And you'll need to invest time tending seedlings and waiting until they reach blooming size (typically one to three years).

Opting to grow perennials from seed can provide the advantage of a fairly wide selection. But some perennial varieties are sterile and thus cannot be grown from seed. Others won't come true from seed—the seedlings do not replicate all the parent plant's traits. Such plants are obtained only as divisions or rooted cuttings.

PERENNIALS FROM FRIENDS

You can find perennials to divide in friends' gardens and at community or garden club

The aster (center) is an ideal transplant. Its roots just fill the soil mix. The variegated obedient plant (left) is pot-bound. With all its root growth massed at the bottom of the pot, it may establish slowly. The coral bells (right) is poorly rooted. Its root ball is likely to crumble during planting, which will damage the roots.

plant exchanges. Such divisions are often far larger specimens than you could buy. You may have the opportunity to talk to the gardener who grew the plant about how large it will be and how it will perform in your environment.

Another plus: Divisions are almost always field grown—taken from outdoor beds. They're in tune with the prevailing weather in your area, whereas plants grown in greenhouses or in other states may require hardening off before planting (see page 15).

Selection at exchanges is limited. Many of the plants spread aggressively; they are available because the mother plant needs curtailment or frequent division. Long-lived, clump-forming species, such as peonies and false indigo, are shared less often.

Bear in mind that problems may move with the plant. Professionally grown plants are cleaner because growers have greater ability to keep plants free of insects and diseases. In the case of soil-dwelling problems, such as crown rot, verticillium wilt, and nematodes, pros can fumigate potting soil, a tactic not usually practical in a home garden.

Even the best garden-grown specimens host some pests. It's prudent to rinse soil off a division before taking it home and to keep that plant under a watchful eye once you've replanted it.

SELECTION TIPS

With so many plants available, how can you choose confidently? Don't focus your attention on flowers. Instead, judge the plant by its leaves, roots, and eyes.

LEAVES: These should be uniformly green, unblemished, and at least as large as your references indicate—all signs of good nutrition and low stress. Such plants will move smoothly into a garden. Avoid plants with limp leaves or dried, brown leaf edges, which are marks of improper watering and poor health.

CAREFUL SELECTION ENSURES SUCCESS—BEAUTIFULLY
continued

Check the roots before buying a plant. Be wary if they don't adequately fill the pot. It means the plant hasn't had the time or conditions to root well.

planting when the soil mix shifts. The broken roots will be prone to fungal infection and will need time for healing before new growth can commence.

EYES: An eye on a perennial is a bud on the roots that's ready to grow into a shoot. Each eye may produce a single stem or a cluster of leaves and a flowering stalk. The number of eyes is directly related to the plant's health and how much energy it stored during the previous growing season. The more eyes on a plant, the bigger—and more quickly— it will grow.

WHAT SIZE TO BUY?

People are often tempted to seek the largest plants available. Usually, this is unnecessary. Many perennials spend much of their first season establishing roots in a bed and they show little increase in size. But if they establish quickly, they can double or triple in size by the second season. Perennials in smaller pots often do just that. They can match and even surpass bigger counterparts because their roots grow more quickly out of the potting soil and into the bed.

If your shopping list includes slow-growing species, look for them in larger sizes. Plants that will be the stars of a garden may also be worth pursuing in larger sizes. Otherwise, focus on the health and vigor of the plants rather than on pot size.

GROWTH RATE: Perennials produce more energy than they use and store the extra to fuel next year's growth. Fast-growing perennials such as Shasta daisies can double or triple in mass and number of flowers by their second year, and then as three-year-old plants reach four to six times the size they were at planting. Longer-lived plants like goatsbeard and hosta take longer to reach the maximum spread and show depicted in catalogs.

The number of eyes (growing points) on a bare-root perennial or division tells how many stems will come.

ROOTS: Gently slide the plant partway out of its pot to check root condition. Roots should be firm, like fresh, crisp vegetables. They should just fill the pot, binding the soil mix together but not circling the sides and bottom in a dense pot-bound layer.

Pot-bound plants do not transplant as well as others because their root tips are all massed at the bottom so there are fewer root tips on the sides. That means the plant has fewer points to grow out of the potting soil and into the garden soil.

Also, watch for loose soil mix shifting away from the root mass when you tip the pot. Such a plant is too small for its pot and price tag, and its root ends are likely to shear off at

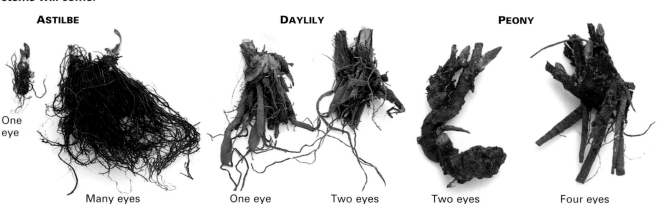

ASTILBE   DAYLILY   PEONY

One eye   Many eyes   One eye   Two eyes   Two eyes   Four eyes

PLANTING THE PERENNIAL BED

Well-planted perennials thrive. These have room to grow; they're not planted too low or too high in the ground, and each one has a watering crater.

Perennials can be planted any time of year, but make the strongest start if planted when the air is cool and the soil warm and moist. Cool air retards top growth while moist, warm soil stimulates rooting, allowing plants to establish wide, drought-resistant, stem-stabilizing bases.

The best times of year to plant are midspring when weeping cherries, forsythia, and Dutch hyacinths are in full bloom, and early autumn before leaf fall when 'Autumn Joy' sedum and perennial fountain grass have passed from flower to seed.

Overcast and drizzly days are ideal for planting. Avoid the middle of a hot day—when water from leaves is lost more quickly than it can be replaced. Even if no permanent damage is done, recovering from wilt consumes energy that the plant could have used to push roots into the new site.

If you must plant in the hot sun, erect shade screens. Plant into moist, friable soil and water each plant immediately afterward.

HARDENING OFF PERENNIALS

When Northerners vacation in the Tropics or lowlanders visit high altitudes, they must gradually acclimate to intense sun or thinner air. Plants are no different. Perennials grown in a greenhouse without wind, wide temperature swings, or direct sun need hardening off—time and stimulus to toughen cell walls and readjust fluid levels so they don't break, dry up, or burn outdoors.

Not every perennial requires hardening. Transplants between outdoor beds don't usually need it. Because garden soil will insulate new bare-root perennials, they can be planted right away, even if 32° F weather is likely. Leaves on the transplant and shoots from the bare roots are tough from the start.

Perennials that have been in a dark package in the mail and those sold from inside a greenhouse in early spring are not ready to be planted. When buying perennials from an outdoor sales area, ask whether they have been hardened off or simply moved out each day from indoors.

If the plants need hardening off, place them in a spot protected from the wind and out of the midday sun for a day. At night, cover them against rapid cooling or move them into a protected area—near the house or in a shed, for example. The next day, give the plants an additional hour of late-morning or midafternoon sun. Protect them again at night. Increase the light and expose them to wind over two more days before planting.

PLANT SPACING IS KEY

Before digging, set the perennials in the bed or mark the bed where each plant will grow; adjust their spacing based on their mature widths. This is also your chance to adjust their arrangement so that the bed looks aesthetically pleasing from the beginning.

It may seem your new perennials are too far apart. But resist the urge to plant them closer. Otherwise, you'll be forced to thin or divide the plants after only a year. Also, avoid filling between perennials with annuals; this not only reduces the water and nutrients available to each plant, but discourages their root growth. Because perennial tops usually grow only as wide as their roots spread the preceding year, temporary fillers may actually

PLANTING THE PERENNIAL BED
continued

Match the digging tool to the pot: a trowel for a 3-inch pot, a small spade for a 4-inch container, and a standard spade, square or round point, to plant large clumps and 8-inch or larger pots.

preserve gaps and delay the garden's maturity.

To minimize the bare look, you can move all plants in a drift (a grouping of one kind of perennial) fractionally closer together. This tactic widens the spaces between different plant types. Such spacing creates an attractive outline of each plant grouping. It also gives you room to work in the garden without stepping on and compressing soil above new roots.

Some gardeners lay out the garden by setting out potted plants. Others place a stake or marker where each perennial will grow. Some even use markers of varied colors and heights to match the expected show. You might draw lines and even a planting key with bonemeal or flour to outline locations of plant groups. Each technique gives you the chance to visualize the garden and make changes before planting.

THE RIGHT PLANTING TOOLS

When you're ready to plant, select the best tool. Match the size of the tool—trowel, spade, or shovel—to the size of the holes needed. A trowel is best for cell packs up to 4-inch pots. Use a shovel or spade for small bare-root plants. Once you spread the roots wide for planting, they will probably need a bigger hole than you first thought.

DON'T PLANT TOO DEEP

Most roots grow horizontally or at a gentle downward angle, so it's better to dig wide rather than straight-down holes. If you disturb the soil beneath the plant too much, the plant may struggle or die as it sinks with the settling subsoil.

If you loosened the whole bed during soil preparation, simply dig holes as wide as the pots (or root spread of bare-root perennials). But if you didn't work the bed because the soil was loose enough to begin with, or you plan to loosen it gradually by sheet composting, dig slope-sided holes twice as wide as the root balls or the roots when spread out. Slope-sided holes yield more rooting area than those with straight sides.

Plant perennials to grow at the same level as they were in the pot or field. With few exceptions, setting perennials too deep invites stem-rot and crown-rot problems. Planting too high (so that the root ball's shoulders are above ground) is also a problem and likely to retard growth. Upper roots grow the most after planting; if they're set high, dry air will check their growth.

Most root growth occurs in oxygen-rich surface layers. So it's a better use of your time and energy to dig wide, slope-sided planting holes than straight-sided holes.

Avoid stress on your wrist: Keep it in the neutral position—in line with the long bones of the arm as if arm and hand were hanging loose at your side.

Don't overstress your knees, back, or wrists. Wear knee pads or kneel on a foam pad. Keep your back straight when bending or lifting. Bend at your hips or knees.

To figure out the proper planting depth for potted perennials, set a still-potted plant into a hole. Check whether it is too high or low. Adjust the hole as needed. If you must return soil to the hole, tamp it well to prevent settling.

Determining the proper planting depth for bare-root perennials requires garden savvy. If the plant tag doesn't have specific directions, look at the color of shoots (eyes) and stems, if any, on the root mass. White or pink shoots and eyes were below ground before and should be covered to about an inch deep again. Where an eye shows green, it was receiving sunlight and should be just above the ground. Stain on stems likely marks the ground level. If there are no visible eyes or stem stains to offer clues, position the root mass so it's barely covered to about 1 inch below ground.

HANDLE ROOTS GENTLY

Handle root balls carefully as you remove the pot. Avoid lifting a plant out of the pot by pulling on its stems. Instead, invert the pot, support the soil on your spread fingers or hands, and lift the pot off the root ball. When a pot will not slide easily, invert the pot and rap it sharply on its rim while supporting the weight of the soil. If the container is flexible, you can roll it on a hard surface to separate root mass from pot. Or cut off the pot.

If you happen to buy a pot-bound plant, it will require some tough love at planting time. In other words, you'll have to injure the plant to promote the best root growth. Otherwise, the roots will probably grow only from the

Dig a planting hole at least as wide as the spread-out roots of your bare-root perennial. Soak bare-root perennials in a bucket of water to moisten any dry roots.

HANDLE WITH CARE

Some perennials transplant without a hitch, others bear a bit of watching after a move to prevent wilting or blowing over in the wind. Still others sulk, even after being moved with the greatest care. Here are some examples from each group. For the rest, look to the "Plant Gallery."

EASY: Daylily, hosta, lady's mantle, daisy, coreopsis, Siberian iris, ornamental grasses
AVERAGE (watch for wilt or windthrow): Astilbe, turtlehead, bearded iris, obedient plant
HARD: Yellow corydalis, monkshood, Japanese anemone, gas plant, false indigo, blue flax, ornamental mullein

PLANTING THE PERENNIAL BED
continued

When unpotting a perennial, spread your fingers around the stems to support the soil's weight. Invert the pot and lift it off with your other hand.

Check the depth as you plant. The top of the root ball should be level with the soil surface.

When roots are badly pot-bound, butterfly the roots. Slice up into the root ball from the bottom and spread the roots wide across mounded soil.

Plant bare-root perennials with their eyes barely covered or within an inch of the surface. Make a mound of soil in the hole and spread the bare roots over it.

bottom of the root ball. So be assertive. Slice off the bottom layer of roots and score the sides vertically in several places. After taking time to repair its injuries, the plant will develop new roots at each point where the roots were severed.

Another technique for handling pot-bound plants is to butterfly the roots. Slice once, vertically into the root mass from the bottom halfway to the top. Spread the two halves over a mound of soil in the planting hole.

Bare roots are deceptive. Having been packed for cold storage or shipping, they lie flat. Soak the roots in water for an hour or two. This replaces water lost in shipping and makes the roots more flexible. Dig a hole at least as wide as the fully spread roots and half as deep as it is wide. Form a sloping mound in the center of the hole, high enough to bring the eyes or stems just at or below ground level. Now splay the roots over this mound. They should be spread wide when planted so the plant is stable in the future and draws water and nutrients from the widest area.

With the plant in the hole or on the mound, begin filling the hole. Tamp to displace air pockets but not so hard as to overly compress the soil. Fill the hole halfway, pat the soil with your hands, water to settle any air pockets, and finish filling.

Use excavated soil to fill in around new plants. Avoid using special soil as backfill, a practice that has been proven to discourage the wide rooting of healthy perennials.

Plants will root best if both the original root ball and the earth around it stay moist throughout the first growing season. So build a watering crater to trap and hold rain and irrigation water until they soak into that vital area. Scrape excess soil into a circular levee about 1 inch high, ringing the entire perennial plus 2 to 3 inches of soil beyond the root ball or farthest spread root.

Now water again, filling the crater. Repair any washouts. Whenever you water, the crater will trap a full ration for the roots below.

KEEP ROOTS MOIST

While perennials become established, irrigate with a watering can or a hose-end shower wand. Both devices let you target individual plants; the craters prevent wasteful runoff to unplanted areas. Desirable perennials grow, whereas areas between perennials stay dry enough to discourage weeds.

New perennials dry out more quickly than established plants. That's because their potted root balls are artificially narrow and have been pampered in terms of watering and fertilizer. Their roots can't sustain their oversized tops with normal irrigation. Water carefully until you see vigorous new growth, a sign that roots are growing out.

NO FERTILIZER NEEDED

Don't rush to fertilize new perennials. In preparing the bed, you've ensured the plants have all needed nutrients. However, if you didn't follow those steps and plants need to be fed, use a slow-release fertilizer until the plant begins strong new growth. Water-soluble nitrogen can soften roots and make them more susceptible to soil-borne diseases.

A new plant may need more than water, sun, and nutrients. Beneficial microorganisms, such as fungi and bacteria, regularly attach themselves to roots. They give roots an increased water-collecting area in exchange for carbohydrates. The plant becomes established quicker. Light-colored soil or soil so compacted before preparation that it was airless may lack beneficial microorganisms. In this case, use products such as Plant Success, MycorTree, or MycoRise.

APPLY A BLANKET OF MULCH

All plantings profit from mulch, which is any material that covers the ground, conserving moisture, moderating soil temperature, and suppressing weeds by shading out weed seeds.

Apply a blanket of mulch to cover the whole bed, including watering craters, but leave a bare ring an inch or two out from the crown of each perennial. Mulch resting against perennial stems can trap heat and moisture there, and rot the stems.

Spread woody mulch, such as bark or composted ground wood, 1 to 2 inches deep. Spread leafy mulches and hulls, such as shredded leaves, pine straw, cocoa hulls, and peanut shells, 2 to 3 inches deep.

ANTICIPATE THE LEANERS

Moist, secure, and blanketed, most perennials need no more special attention. A few may benefit from staking. For example, a spring-planted bearded iris may bloom before its roots spread far enough to anchor the heavy blossom. If the plant topples, it can uproot itself. Spring-planted peony, delphinium, blazing star, cardinal flower, and beard-tongue may also have trouble supporting their first flowers. Any large-flowered species is at risk if forced into early bloom—which many garden centers do to stimulate early sales.

To prevent toppling, place a stake next to each main stem, driving it into undisturbed soil under the plant. Tie the stems to the stakes as they grow.

Directing water into the craters around new perennials ensures that irrigation water won't run away from the roots until it has had a chance to soak in.

Spread mulch up to and over the rim of the watering crater, but avoid letting it rest against the plant stems.

If you must plant in the hot sun, shade the plants during the hottest part of the day for a week or two. This shade is dark cloth attached to stakes.

WATERING NEW PERENNIALS

1ST DAY Plant and water the perennials.
IN 2 DAYS Three days after planting, check soil moisture; water again if it's drying down. Fill watering crater. If water soaks in immediately, fill crater again until the water soaks in gradually.
IN 3 MORE DAYS Check soil moisture and water if soil is drying down.
IN 4 MORE DAYS Check, water as needed.
IN 5 MORE DAYS Check and water as needed.
IN 6 MORE DAYS Check and water as needed.
IN 7 MORE DAYS Twenty-eight days after planting, the perennials are on schedule for weekly water checks, the same as the rest of the garden.

Weeding and edging are important parts of day-to-day care in a perennial garden. Edging provides a crisp look and can prevent weeds from invading a bed.

Removing faded flowers is called deadheading. This activity keeps a garden neat, stimulates plants to produce additional blooms, and can help prevent some diseases. By preventing seed set, deadheading also cuts down on "volunteer" perennials which may become weeds.

DAY-TO-DAY CARE

When you match perennials to the site, prepare the soil well, and plant carefully, a perennial garden may need little maintenance. But there is no such thing as a no-maintenance garden, so refer to this chapter to keep your new bed in good shape.

The activities listed here appear in order of importance. If you take care of those that are most important, at least some of the other work takes care of itself. For instance, if watering and weeding are done well, the plants will be healthy enough to resist trouble so there are fewer pests for you to control. Plants that are well watered and free of weedy competition have stronger stems so there is less need for staking. If you are unfamiliar with perennial care, start with the first item here—watering—and master that before spending too much time on staking, grooming, or dividing, which you'll find later in the chapter.

Dividing plants is essential. It ensures perennials maintain their "youth" so that they grow most vigorously, bloom best, and are most resistant to pests.

WATERING

Rotary and oscillating sprinklers are good for covering large areas and rinsing off dusty foliage

Watering cans and shower wands are efficient for filling watering craters of new plantings quickly.

Drip irrigation systems and weeper hoses conserve water while wetting the soil and keeping foliage dry.

Professional growers put only experienced employees in charge of watering. They know how much water plants need, how to measure it, and when to adjust amounts and techniques. Here are the secrets to watering plants like a pro.

HOW MUCH TO WATER?

Perennials need an average of 1 to 2 inches of water per week. How do you know if you apply that much?

To measure the output of a sprinkler, let it fill a rain gauge to the 1-inch mark, or use a straight-sided container, such as a tuna can. This may take 15 minutes to six hours, depending on water pressure, hose length, sprinkler type, size of area, wind, and evaporation rate.

To measure the output of a drip or weeper line, check the soil 1 foot from an emitter or the far end of the hose. One inch of water wets soil 3 to 4 inches deep, which may take several hours. Dig down that far with a trowel. If the soil feels cool, it is moist and it has received 1 inch of water.

You also can tell when to water by feeling the soil several inches down. If it feels warm, it is dry so watering is needed.

UNDERSTAND THE SITE

Every site has unique wet and dry areas. A bed catching overthrow from a neighbor's sprinklers won't need as much water as beds under rain-blocking eaves or next to brick walls, which wick away moisture. Check all beds regularly until you know which are the first and last to dry out. Use those as indicator beds when deciding whether to water.

Several conditions affect watering frequency and technique. The illustration on page 23 demonstrates how water needs can vary across a landscape.

RAIN: Monitor weather reports or check the rain gauge, then water each week to make up the difference. In large plantings, use several rain gauges to ensure all beds receive an inch of rain.

SOIL TYPE: One inch of water may keep clay moist for more than a week, but excessively drained sandy soils may need frequent light waterings totaling more than 1 inch per week.

SOIL CONDITION: Infiltration rate—how quickly moisture seeps into soil pores—may be slow on compacted soil and on slopes. Some silty soils repel water if they're dry. Compensate by watering slowly, or do it in spurts, stopping when water begins to run off, restarting after it soaks in. Use a mulch; it collects water, preventing runoff.

PLANTS: Some perennials sulk if denied water for a day; others like it dry. Most fall in between. For easy maintenance, group perennials by their particular watering needs.

CRITICAL WATERING TIMES

Plants are needier at some times than others, especially when growing rapidly. If they dry down in early spring, they may be weak all season, even species that can normally shrug off weeks of summer drought.

It's important to water in fall, when perennials aren't growing many leaves but are adding roots at a rapid rate. Moisture in fall can greatly improve the next year's show.

New plants dry out more quickly than perennials with wide, established root systems. Regularly check newly planted perennials during the first season, with watering can in hand.

THE BEST TIME TO WATER

Water in the early morning for the best results. At first light, the air is calm and plants take up water rapidly so there's little waste. The foliage dries quickly as the air warms and breezes stir. This thwarts leaf diseases that thrive on damp leaves and high humidity.

There are exceptions to morning irrigation. In hot, dry regions where water is scarce, nighttime irrigation cuts losses to evaporation. Risk of infection is not significant, because humidity-loving leaf diseases are suppressed by the very dry air.

Some plants, especially recent transplants, may need midday watering to cool the air and prevent wilt. You might water at every opportunity if you're helping certain plants recover from stress, such as heavy insect infestation or hailstorm damage.

In the final analysis, when the soil is dry and plants need water, turn on the sprinklers, regardless of the hour.

Those who base watering on rainfall and soil moisture know that it may not be needed every week. In some regions, it may be necessary only four or five times a year. Where perennial gardens are extensive, watering may take hours and run around the clock. The infrequency of such evening and nighttime shifts makes them no more risky than late-night rains.

WAYS TO WATER

Choose the watering system—overhead or direct-to-soil, automatic or manual—ideally suited to the site and your needs.

Overhead systems cleanse foliage, keeping dust-related problems and mite damage low. Their output is easily measured, and the systems are readily available in many forms. But your plants are at increased risk of leaf diseases, runoff on windy and hilly sites, and battered foliage if plants grow across a spray path.

Direct-to-soil watering conserves water and keeps foliage dry, but you may have difficulty measuring amounts applied or remembering to be vigilant with drip lines and weepers. In such invisible flows, clogs can go unnoticed until plants downstream wilt.

An automatic system frees you from wrestling with hoses. But it may lull you into checking soil moisture less often. Overwatering and dry corners may go unnoticed.

A manual system with overhead and direct-to-soil elements plus semiautomatic extras may be best for perennials. Most botanical gardens employ these hybrid systems in perennial areas.

SPECIAL CASES

Downslope

A–Low area: Don't overwater; runoff from higher areas keeps it wet.
B–Severe slope: Water slowly or in short frequent spurts to avoid run off. If the slope faces south, sun dries soil; check moisture often.
C–Under trees: Check soil moisture often; tree roots quickly take up excess water.
D–Wind tunnel: Use drip system or hand water to ensure all plants receive water because wind distorts sprinkler pattern.

FERTILIZING

Fertilize perennials to support faster growth and larger flowers, to replace nutrients lost in weeding and clipping, and to amend soils that would not normally suit the species you want to grow.

FERTILIZERS FOR ACID-LOVING PLANTS

Fertilizers for acid-loving plants contain sulfur and certain nutrients that wouldn't normally be available in alkaline soils. The sulfur produces weak sulfuric acid, which helps dissolve nutrients from soils normally too alkaline to release them. Use these products if you want to grow an acid-loving perennial such as gas plant on very alkaline soil.

You can't rely solely on rainfall for the best perennial show. Nor should you expect nature to supply all nutrients. Gardeners' standards are higher than nature's, and weeding, deadheading, cutting flowers, and removing plant debris disrupt the natural recycling of nutrients. If you grow exotic perennials as well (species not naturally found in your area), your soil may lack minerals they need. You're going to have to fertilize.

WHAT FERTILIZERS DO

Some people believe that fertilizers feed plants and stimulate plant growth. Not true. Plants create their own food through photosynthesis—by making sugars and starches (necessary fuel) from carbon dioxide and water, using the energy of sunlight. Growth and flowering are controlled by temperature, sunlight, water, and internally produced hormones. Fertilizers simply provide essential elements needed by actively growing plants, just as vitamins help humans build strong bones and have a healthy glow.

Generally, to ensure essential elements are available, fertilize when perennials first start growing each year and again when flower buds begin to form. Ideally, you would fertilize each plant on its own schedule, because each species starts to grow and flower at different times—cool-season perennials first, later-emerging species weeks or months later. However, most gardens contain dozens of species, and most gardeners have dozens of other priorities. So the best compromise is to fertilize to meet average growth and blooming peaks.

FERTILIZER SCHEDULE

Roots have no teeth and so can't chew fertilizer pellets or bits of rock phosphate. The only nutrient a root can use is one dissolved in water. Fertilizers applied in solution, such as Miracle-Gro, are immediately usable. But they will leach out of the root zone as rain and irrigation water move through soil. So it's best to use such products biweekly or monthly in small doses from the time your plants begin to grow until their foliage matures.

Products such as sulfur- or polymer-coated urea (Osmocote) dissolve very slowly. Nutrient-rich organic materials, such as manure or fish meal, must decompose before dissolving. The nutrients in slow-release fertilizers become available to plants gradually over a long period. With them, you can apply all or most of the season's ration in one application in late fall or midspring, one to three months before plants will use it.

A hybrid schedule suits many plants and gardeners. A slow-release product may be applied once a year and supplemented with

HEAVY FEEDERS

■ Astilbe
■ Clematis
■ Delphinium
■ Peony

Pale older leaves (lower ones), smaller-than-normal leaves, and thin stems indicate nitrogen need.

LIGHT FEEDERS

■ Artemisia
■ Barrenwort
■ Mullein

Weak stems, reduced flowering, and rank growth may indicate too much nitrogen has been applied near the plants.

WHEN TO FERTILIZE

The type of fertilizer you use will govern when how often you need to fertilize as well as how much to apply.

Fertilizer Type	When to Apply	Examples	Amount 100 sq. ft.	10 sq. ft.
Quick-release powders (Dissolves in water; immediately available)	Mix according to label directions and sprinkle over garden when large daffodils are in bloom or when flower buds forming; reapply every two weeks.	15-30-15 10-52-10 30-10-10	2⅔ cups 2⅔ cups 01⅓ cups	4½ tbsp. 4½ tbsp. 2 tbsp.
Standard granular (Nitrogen available to plants soon after applied)	Apply at two week intervals until full amount has been applied. Or scratch half the total into soil surface in spring one most plants in bed have begun to grow. Repeat in late spring when Siberian irises are in full bloom.	12-12-12 5-10-5	3 cups 7 cups	5–6 tbsp. ¾ cup
Slow-release materials (Nitrogen released when soil is warm and moist. Available to plants for two to three months. Synthetic granular fertilizer)	Synthetic granular product: Scratch entire amount into soil surface in spring as bulb foliage emerges. Natural or organic fertilizer: Scratch half into the soil surface in early spring as bulb foliage emerges; repeat in autumn when tree leaves fall	14-14-14 5-5-5	2½ cups 10⅔ cups	4 tbsp. 1 cup

Use in the absence of soil test results. Amounts shown will provide nitrogen at the rate of 2 pounds of nitrogen per 1,000 square feet per year. Some perennials may need more or less than that per year (see the "Plant Gallery" for guidelines. A soil test will tell you which fertilizer formula is best to provide the appropriate amounts of phosphorus and potassium for your garden. (tbsp. stands for tablespoon)

faster-acting, more concentrated, water-soluble products as foliage color and other plant responses dictate.

CHOOSING A FERTILIZER

The major nutrients provided by most fertilizers are nitrogen (N), phosphorus (P), and potassium (K). Phosphorus and potassium are minerals; nitrogen comes from rainwater and decomposing organic matter.

A soil test will tell you the nutrients available in your soil and recommend amounts of supplemental fertilizer needed. For instance, soil test results may advise you to use a high-phosphorus fertilizer such as 5-10-5 (5 percent N, 10 percent P, 5 percent K). Check local government directory listings for a county or state Extension Service office near you. Without soil test results to guide your choice of fertilizers, choose one that provides balanced amounts of nitrogen, phosphorus, and potassium, such as 14-14-14.

CALCULATING AMOUNT

How much fertilizer to apply is based on perennials' use of nitrogen. Nitrogen, of the three major nutrients, is a double-edged sword. It is essential to all plant parts in all growth phases, but too much can dehydrate roots and leaf tips, weaken tissues, and encourage insects and disease. You should calculate fertilizers to provide enough but not too much nitrogen.

The average perennial fares well if its bed is fertilized so that 1 pound of actual nitrogen is spread over about 500 square feet. A bag of 10-10-10 contains 10 percent nitrogen, so 10 pounds of that fertilizer is the right amount to work into 500 square feet of bed. Here's how it's figured: 10 percent multiplied by 10 pounds equals 1 pound of nitrogen. Calculations for other fertilizers and smaller areas are provided in the chart above.

HOW TO APPLY FERTILIZERS

Because fertilizer must dissolve to be of use to plants, mix it in water (water-soluble types) or spread it on bare soil and scratch it in (granular and slow-release products).

A good time to spread fertilizer is just before you plan to weed a perennial bed because weeding will help mix the fertilizer into the top inch or two of soil. Scatter granules as evenly as possible across an area. Avoid depositing any on the foliage, where it may cause a contact burn.

Water immediately after fertilizing to dissolve some of the fertilizer and to wash any granules or dust off foliage.

You can opt to use a combination of fertilizers, such as blood meal to supply nitrogen, steamed bonemeal for phosphorus, and greensand for potassium. Use these products long before plants need them, because all are slow-acting. Apply them in three separate passes. Mixing can result in an uneven application of one product or another.

WEEDING AND MULCHING

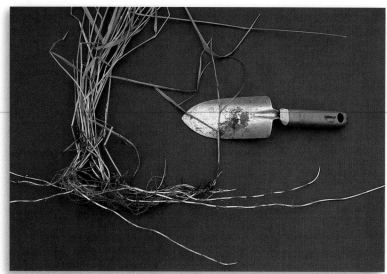

Weeds, such as quackgrass, are trouble for perennial gardeners. They spread on running roots, can live many years, and grow back quickly from tiny pieces of root.

into the light. If you weed every time you pass a bed, you may be tempted to shake the soil from the weed's roots, scattering more seeds. Unless you cover or treat all disrupted and dropped soil, weeds will sprout before your next serious weeding.

KNOW THE ENEMY

Knowledge is power. Know weeds by name, root type, and life cycle—annual, biennial, or perennial—to help keep them at bay. (Learn about specific weeds and how to eliminate or reduce their sources on pages 54 and 55.) Hoe, pull, kill, or smother weeds before they set seed.

HOEING AND PULLING

Hoeing works best when the hoe is sharp, the soil slightly dry, and the seedlings uniformly small. Use a short-handled hoe so that you can get in close to the plants and maintain control of the blade, minimizing nicks to perennial stems.

Pulling, which is time-consuming, is best for removing an occasional overlooked weed and older seedlings that are not easily hoed, killed, or smothered. It's most effective in loose soil, where a tug yields all or most of the roots. Keep beds loose with regular additions of organic matter. Or have a garden fork handy to insert deeply into the ground and loosen the soil as you pull.

Although many gardeners like to work in soil softened by rain, this may cause frustration. When soil is moist during weeding, hoeing only partly dislodges weeds, which soon recover. Any dredged-up weed seeds will fall on moist soil, which makes it likely they will germinate. Also, post-rain weeding removes moisture from a bed. The weeds are full of water that might have been absorbed by the bed's rightful tenants.

Effective weeding begins with a simple, practical definition of *weed:* any plant growing where you don't want it.

Pull weeds not only to eliminate eyesores but to rid the bed of competition for water and nutrients. Eliminating weeds also opens space between plants, which improves air circulation, helps control fungi, and cuts down on places where pests can hide.

BIWEEKLY OR MONTHLY WEEDING

For best weed control, plant into a clean bed. Keep it clean with regular pulling or hoeing, and use a mulch layer or preemergence herbicide to suppress weed seedlings.

Weed every two weeks during a bed's first season. Weed thoroughly, then renew the mulch or preemergent wherever you disturbed the soil. In time, fewer new seedlings will sprout in each two-week interval, and weeding once a month will suffice in the second and subsequent years.

Avoid weeding more frequently; pulling out weeds brings subsurface, dormant weed seeds

Identify your weeds so you will know how they spread. Then locate and block the source. Weeds most commonly spread by running roots, seeds, or both.

KILLING ANNUAL OR BIENNIAL WEEDS

Herbicide is one way to kill annual and biennial weeds. You can kill weeds by smothering—that is, by blocking light and physically preventing the weeds from finding their way to the sun's rays. Smother very small seedlings under 2 inches of mulch. You may have to flatten older weeds

Take care with herbicides. Use a barrier, such as a piece of cardboard, to protect desirable plants from splashes, drips, or drifting spray.

Spot treat by painting herbicides on weed foliage. Be sure the product dries before allowing adjacent perennials to touch treated weeds.

This large can keeps herbicide spray contained, protecting nearby perennials. Spray through a hole in the can bottom.

under newspaper weighted with 2 inches or more of mulch. The newspaper eventually decomposes.

Select an herbicide, such as glyphosate (Roundup), that leaves no residue in the soil to affect remaining plants and that kills roots after being absorbed through the leaves. Apply herbicide carefully, only on calm days. Always shield desirable perennials from overspray or herbicide dripping off a brush.

SUPPRESS NEW SEEDLINGS

After removing annual and biennial weeds, suppress new seedlings by applying a preemergence weed killer or putting down a blanket of mulch. You can spread a preemergence herbicide, such as trifluralin (Treflan) or corn gluten meal (A-Maizing Lawn), on bare soil. Scratch it lightly into the top inch to kill weed seeds as they sprout. Preemergents should not normally affect established perennials.

Use preemergents only as directed on the package label and only in places and seasons when weeds have been a problem. They have the potential to reach levels harmful to sensitive perennials in dry years and in some types of soil.

Two inches of mulch also stops many weed seeds from sprouting. The layer denies them light or keeps them so far under cover that the seedlings exhaust their reserves and die before reaching light.

Where it is 2 inches deep, mulch may be 100 percent effective. But where it must taper off near crowns of perennials, it is less so. If mulch is your weed prevention strategy,

be vigilant about weeding under the skirts of perennials.

Whether you choose to apply preemergence herbicide or mulch, time it for your weeds' life cycle. Warm-season species, such as crabgrass and purslane, germinate in mid- to late spring. You can prevent them by having the herbicide or mulch in place by midspring.

Cool-season weeds, such as chickweed and tall rocket, germinate in fall, late winter, or very early spring, then grow so rapidly that they'll often be in bloom by your first midspring visit to the bed. Where cool-season weeds are common, apply preemergence herbicide or mulch at fall cleanup.

Weeding tools should suit both you and the weeds. Long handles can spare your knees, but short handles provide better control close to perennial crowns. Choose hoes to battle seedlings; use spading forks or grubbers for deeper-rooted weeds.

WEEDING AND MULCHING
continued

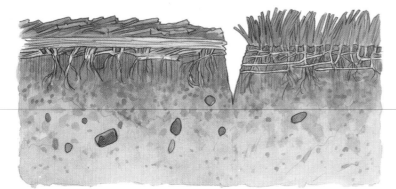

Smothering is usually effective if the weeds are covered during at least two months of their most active growing season.

WEEDS: CLUMPER OR RUNNER?

Some perennial weeds form clumps. Others have running roots at, near, or far below the soil surface. (This trait is identified for each perennial weed in the "Troubleshooting" chapter on page 54.) As you meet new weeds, including once-desirable perennials that proved to be weedy, check the roots to know what you're up against.

CLUMPERS: Clump-forming perennials, such as dandelions or plantains, may have a root that can generate a new top; their clumping nature keeps them stationary. Remove as much of their root as possible. Use a garden fork to loosen deeply next to the weed, then pull.

Alternatively, treat clump-formers or any perennial weed with glyphosate (Roundup) or a similar product. Work when the weed's foliage is lush so it absorbs a large dose.

Preemergent weed killer spread evenly on the soil surface kills weed seeds as they sprout. Used as directed, it is not usually harmful to plants.

After pulling or killing the weed, monitor for resurgence from surviving root tissue. It's not unusual to pull or treat a well-established perennial weed three or four times before its reserves are exhausted. Always mulch an area bared by weed removal; that bare soil is likely to be full of seeds from the plant removed.

HOW TO REMOVE RUNNING ROOTS:

Perennial weeds with running roots include grasses, mint, and artemisia. Loosen the soil with a garden fork everywhere you see sprouts of these plants. Then remove them, beginning at the center of the colony and working out to the newest shoots. This may be the only way to find and remove runners that have not yet sent shoots to the surface. Where the runners infiltrate desirable perennials' crowns, loosen the soil and pursue them into that stronghold, even if this means lifting the perennial.

Killing running-root perennials with herbicide can be tedious. You must check the area every few days to treat shoots that emerge after the application. Several follow-up sprays may be required, and any long delay between these visits may give weeds time to regenerate and prolong the battle.

Sprouts often surface within the crowns of desirable perennials where weed killer cannot be applied. Then it's best to dig up the perennial to remove the running root.

The hardest perennial weeds to eliminate have running roots that go deep and wide, such as quackgrass and bindweed. If you see such a plant in an area before planting, allow extra time between preparation and planting—even several seasons—to be sure the bed is clean. If such weeds are established in a bed or have invaded it from surrounding areas, your only options are repeated digging, or killing with herbicide and follow-ups every few days. Even these tough weeds will shrink and die in a season or two if you are faithful to a follow-up schedule.

MULCH AS WEED CONTROL

Mulching a weed-free bed not only keeps the bed clean, it has other benefits. It prevents rapid heating or cooling of the soil, thereby allowing steady root growth. It reduces evaporative water loss. If an organic material is used as mulch, its particles become soil-enriching humus as they decompose. In addition, a well-chosen mulch with a color and texture complementary to the perennials can make the whole bed more attractive.

Many materials can be used as mulch. Select one that is the color and texture you prefer, is readily available, and fits your garden budget. Also consider scent—some people like the odor of ground fir bark or cocoa hulls; others don't.

The best perennial mulches are organic materials that will decompose between 12 and 18 months after application. Once broken

Until the perennial expands to cover the area around its crown, weed seeds are likely to sprout in this no-mulch area. Be sure to weed under the skirts of perennials until they have filled out.

Loosen the soil; use a spade to slice through the densest part of the colony; lift a section at a time to establish its root depth. Holding the most thickly rooted section in one hand, loosen under the roots to 'chase' every runner out from its source.

MUCH MISUNDERSTANDING ABOUT MULCH

MYTH 1: Rake away mulch in spring to allow soil to warm up.

This is a misconception based on English practice. In cool, mild climates and areas so far north that spring sun is at a very low angle, removing the mulch may hasten warming. But in most of the U.S. continent, soil temperatures rise rapidly in spring even under mulch.

MYTH 2: Don't mulch in fall until the soil freezes.

No need to wait. Apply mulch anytime the existing material is too thin to suppress seed germination. If you apply a very heavy mulch to protect crowns during the winter (see page 43), do it after freezing air temperatures have stopped top growth. Where voles are a problem, waiting until the soil freezes can stop them from taking up residence in the mulch and feeding on the crowns over winter.

MYTH 3: Salt-marsh hay is the best mulch for perennials.

Every region has its traditional, preferred, or most readily available mulches. Salt-marsh hay is no better as a mulch than any of a dozen other regional favorites. Gardening books written by Northeastern gardeners in the mid-1900s popularized salt-marsh hay, and its mythical reputation lives on.

MYTH 4: Oak leaf and pine needle mulches are so acidic they kill plants.

Stop worrying. Almost all organic mulches affect soil pH as they break down. Oak and pine foliage are two that produce a slightly acid reaction. They are not useful where soil is already very acid and you wish to raise the pH, but in slightly acid to very alkaline soils they are excellent mulches. The notion that pine needles kill plants may be related to the barren earth often found under pines. This absence of vegetation usually has more to do with the lack of water under a pine than the soil pH, which may be alkaline despite decades of needle fall. Oak leaves contain tannic acid, which is said to leach into standing water. Plant failure probably occurs because of poor drainage rather than low pH.

MYTH 5: Mulch must be worked into the soil as it breaks down.

Unnecessary. Once mulch is decomposed enough that it is no longer recognizable, allow it to mix into the soil during weeding or other garden work, but don't make a special effort to incorporate it. Soil organisms, such as earthworms, will do that for you with far greater effect and less trauma to plant roots.

MYTH 6: If mulch is added every year, the soil level in a bed increases rapidly.

Two to 3 inches of mulch decompose to roughly $\frac{1}{4}$ inch of compost, which degrades into humus and water-soluble nutrients. Plants take up the nutrients to incorporate into their tissues. So we remove the remains of last year's mulch every time we remove plant matter in weeding, dividing, or general cleaning up. New mulch usually adds only enough material to replace what's lost in this cycle.

MYTH 7: Mulch attracts termites.

Not true. There is no evidence that termites are attracted to mulched areas. Mulch does contribute to cool, moist, rich soil, which will sustain more life of all kinds than dry, worn-out soil. Such variety and quantity of creatures is a sign of fertile soil and is usually self-regulating, in that predator organisms in the soil will act to keep any pest populations in check.

MYTH 8: Weed barrier cloth hidden under bark is an excellent mulch for perennials.

Dead wrong. Plastic and woven "weed barriers" do not effectively curb weeds. Weeds grow in decaying mulch on top of the barriers. Barrier cloths do not allow clumps of perennials to increase in size, cost more than mulch alone, and decrease the amount of oxygen in the soil, which lowers soil fertility. Plastic mulches stop air movement into the soil; weed barrier cloth reduces the activity of worms tunneling between the soil surface and the subsoil, which indirectly decreases soil oxygen.

WEEDING AND MULCHING
continued

CHOOSE A MULCH

Mulch	Properties	Other notes
Shredded, chipped, or processed bark	Brown; darkness varies; smallest particle size tends to be darkest, but widely variable so look before you buy if color matters. Coarse to fine in texture, widely variable. Bark can deplete nitrogen in soil as it decomposes; little effect on pH.	All bark and wood products may bring slime mold with them; it is rarely harmful but is unsightly.
Chipped wood	Gray-white to light brown; often fades to much paler color. Medium texture. Can deplete nitrogen in soil as it decomposes; little effect on pH.	Not recommended. May consist of recycled wood colored with vegetable dye, which leaches. Wood containing copper or arsenic, such as pressure-treated lumber, may have herbicidal properties.
Sawdust	Yellow to white; fine texture. Can deplete nitrogen in soil as it decomposes; little effect on pH.	Cultivate regularly; otherwise fungal strands can web particles together and block water absorption.
Hulls: cocoa bean, pecan, buckwheat, peanut	Color and texture vary. Often supply nutrients as they decompose. Less likely to tie up nitrogen than wood products; neutral to acidifying effect on pH.	Availability varies.
Residue: spent hop, ground corncob	Color and texture vary. May supply nutrients as it decomposes; neutral to acidifying effect on soil pH.	Acquaint yourself with the odor of these mulches before selecting one.
Yard waste, compost, spent mushroom compost	Very dark brown to black-brown; fine texture. May supply nutrients. Neutral to acidifying effect on pH.	Test pH and soluble salts. Extremely alkaline compost with high-soluble salts is common and may stunt perennial growth. Check cleanliness by sifting for pieces of weed roots; then fill a pot with compost, moisten it, and watch for weed seedlings.
Leaves: deciduous tree leaves or pine needles	Color varies from light brown to yellow; texture varies. Supply nutrients as they decompose; neutral to acidifying effect on pH.	May include seeds. Appearance is best if shredded. Largest, slowest-decaying leaves such as sycamore, oak, and Norway maple can mat unless shredded. Pine needles can be slippery underfoot.
Stones	Color and texture vary. Rarely supply nutrients. Limestone increases pH.	Not recommended among perennials since they get in the way whenever you need to disturb the soil.
Chicken grit	Gray color; fine texture. No nutrient value. Little effect on pH.	For perennials intolerant of moist soil pressing against foliage or crown, or for windy and rooftop beds where lighter mulches may blow away.
Turface	Gray-brown color; medium texture. No effect on nutrients or pH.	For perennials intolerant of moist soil against foliage or crown and windy and rooftop beds where lighter mulches may blow away.
Shredded paper	Color varies; medium texture. Little effect on nutrients. No effect on pH.	Low cost. Avoid use of glossy paper, which may contain toxic inks. Often unattractive and should be covered by a more attractive mulch.
Grass clippings	Pale green to straw color; fine texture. High in nitrogen. Little effect on pH.	Low cost. Apply cool and fresh from mower bag. Don't use on gardens for two weeks after weed killer has been applied to lawn. Must renew more often than most mulches. May contain weed seeds
Cones, spruce or pine	Color varies; texture coarse. Insignificant effect on nutrients or pH.	Economical way to recycle materials. Low cost where conifers are abundant.
Spent soilless potting mix from patio containers	Dark brown; fine texture. No effect on nutrient levels. Acidifying effect on pH.	May promote weed growth.
Coffee grounds, eggshells, other food-preparation castoffs	Color and texture vary. May supply nutrients. Some materials are acidifying, others mildly alkaline.	Economical way to recycle materials. Ask at coffee shops and office building coffee stations about obtaining coffee grounds.

These perennials were planted at the same time but mulched with different materials to demonstrate how a mulch can affect the growth rate. Those grown in high-carbon wood mulch (top left) are smaller.

Fine shredded bark

Coarse shredded bark

Cocoa bean hulls

Processing residue

Compost

Leaf mold

Pine straw

down into earthy-scented, unrecognizable dark crumbs, they can be allowed to mix into the soil during the normal course of garden activities.

Mulches that decompose more rapidly, such as grass clippings, must be renewed as the mulch layer becomes thin and weed seeds begin to sprout. Those that decompose more slowly or not at all—rocks, large wood chunks, or the chips of decay-resistant bark, such as eucalyptus or cypress—may cause extra work for the gardener when dividing perennials, fertilizing, or weeding. That is, those mulches must be moved out of the way and put back later so that they do not mix with the soil as you work.

Do not overmulch. One to 2 inches of wood chips, bark, or stony material is sufficient. Materials that are quicker to break down, such as leaves, cocoa hulls, or compost, can be applied 2 to 3 inches thick.

If piled too deeply initially, grass clippings will rot to a slimy mess then dry to a water-shedding, cardboard-like mat. Spread clippings no more than 2 inches deep at a time; they'll dry without matting. Once dry, you can put another layer on top of the first.

PEST PATROL

Your garden will be free of serious pest problems if you site plants well and keep up on day-to-day chores, including patrolling for pests. Check the color and growth of your plants regularly, and look for early signs of trouble. Inspect new plants weekly during their first season; older plants about once a month.

It's helpful to know what to expect of a healthy perennial. After buying an unfamiliar plant, try to find a healthy established example in a nearby garden. Then keep an eye on it to gauge whether changes in your plant—leaf color and size, growth rate, blemishes—are normal.

Inspect new plants regularly, and established plants once a month. Pay attention to leaf undersides, foliage near the ground, and tip growth to catch the early signs of trouble.

If they're not, check how its growing conditions differ from those of the healthy plant. Is it in more sun or more shade, wetter or drier soil, a windy site or a protected one? Give your plant the same environment and care as the healthy one.

BE ALERT

When patrolling for pests, look closely at the youngest and oldest foliage for signs of insect feeding or disease. Soft new growth is the first to be attacked by some insects and diseases. Other pests thrive among the dense, dark lower and inner leaves. A check of leaf undersides may reveal insects, eggs, or other identifiable disease symptoms. Also look for signs of damage or infection in the roots of an ailing plant. Know all you can about a problem before reaching for a remedy.

This book's "Plant Gallery," *The Ortho Home Gardener's Problem Solver*, or *Diseases* and *Pests of Ornamental Plants* by P. P. Pirone can help you determine how serious a problem is, whether it's likely to get worse or spread to other plants, and when you should take action. Some problems are cosmetic—unsightly but not serious. You can let these run their course unless their population builds up so that control measures become worth the time or expense. Pests that can kill a plant should be dealt with more decisively.

Choose the pest control method suited to your particular desires and schedule. Pest control requires repetition whether you use biological or chemical control

COMPARING PEST CONTROLS

Every pest control method has advantages and disadvantages. Smart gardeners acquaint themselves with the possible side effects of their chosen pesticides, no matter the type. Here is a comparison of a home remedy and a commercial product for two major pesticide categories.

	Effectiveness	Considerations
INSECTICIDE		
Carbaryl (Sevin)	Kills a wide range of pests; residual lasts 7 days or longer	May damage leaves; sticks well. Odor offensive to some. Use caution when handling, mixing, and applying.
Capsaicin (4 tbsp. hot pepper sauce per quart)	Controls many soft-bodied insects; little residual	Material often at hand. Test before use; may burn foliage. Irritates eyes and skin.
FUNGICIDE		
Chlorothalonil	Prevents some fungal diseases; 7–14 day residual	Rarely damages plant. Sticks well. Odor offensive to some. Use caution when handling. Toxic to fish.
Baking soda (1 tbsp. soda + 1 tsp. vegetable oil in 2 quarts water)	Prevents some fungal diseases; lasts until washed off	May burn foliage; test before use. Must be reapplied in wet weather.
MOLLUSCICIDE		
Metaldehyde	Kills any slug that eats it; Effective for 14 days; less in rainy weather	May burn foliage if pellets rest on leaves. Use great caution when handling. Toxic to pets and birds
Ammonia (1 cup in 3 cups water)	Kills slugs on contact; no residual	May burn foliage; rinse after application. Effective only on contact so must be applied when slugs are active (at night or cloudy days). Does not affect slugs it doesn't reach. May irritate eyes, skin, lungs.

methods. If the instructions call for three applications over three weeks, do it. That kills successive generations or residual organisms. Pests could rebound if you don't.

Check the method's effectiveness during your next regular patrol. If it worked, results will show. If the problem recurs, you'll know to alter your approach.

Keep a calendar of problems. For example, if Japanese beetles appear in early July one year, they are likely to do so in future years. Covering the beetles' favorite plants in late June with lightweight floating row cover allows you to bar the beetles or kill them outside the cover before they do damage.

Knowing when certain pests usually appear can also help in handling exceptions. For instance, aphids and other sucking insects proliferate when plants are growing most actively so that soft, moist tissue is abundant—mid- to late spring. If you see aphids in August, you will know it's unusual.

If you find pest problems developing, don't step up pest control measures until it's certain that plant selection, watering, weeding, and fertilization are all appropriate.

MANY WAYS TO CONTROL A PEST

There are always options in pest control. Here are all the basic categories of control, from the narrowest in impact—those most likely to affect only the pest—to the broadest—those more likely to affect plants and organisms beyond the targeted pest. Professional gardeners use this type of ranking when following a procedure called integrated pest management, in which the option that is effective but narrowest in scope is chosen first, and many different methods of control are used in one garden.

Method	Use when	Comments
Psychological control: Gardener adjusts his/her tolerance level and accepts some damage.	Damage is cosmetic in nature or not likely to spread beyond the plant involved.	Continue to patrol in case other problems come up.
Biological control: Encourage or even add natural predators and pathogens such as lady beetles against aphids or scale, predatory nematodes against vine weevil grubs, or the bacteria Bt (*Bacillus thuringiensis*) against caterpillars.	Gardener wishes to have seven-day-a-week, 24-hour-a-day assistance in preventing pests from reaching damaging numbers.	Not usually effective in clearing up pest problems that have already reached damaging levels.
Mechanical control: Handpick insects, install screen barriers or fencing, or use any method that physically removes or bars the pest.	Pests are relatively large and few in number. Prevention rather than cure.	More and more often used in botanical gardens and large nurseries when chemical controls such as repellents prove ineffective. Such large-scale professional use is creating demand for and appearance of products such as handheld suction devices to remove insects and inexpensive plastic fencing to exclude deer.
Cultural control: Change the type of soil, amount of sun, availability or method of applying water, or other maintenance procedure to increase plant health and natural resistance. Replace plants with varieties resistant to the existing pests.	Cost of labor to employ mechanical controls is prohibitive, and there are difficulties in applying chemical controls, as in public gardens where beds cannot be closed while chemicals are applied.	Always look for resistant varieties when selecting perennials. Restrictions on use of pesticides in public areas have increased the demand for and development of resistant varieties.
Chemical control: Use chemical solutions and powders to repel or kill pests. Includes all chemicals, including those found in kitchen cleaning products, mineral powders, oils, and toxins derived from plants, synthesized versions of plant products, and petroleum-based pesticides.	Remedying a pest problem already too large or extensive to address by other methods. Also used where applying a spray or dust is more effective at reaching the pests than other methods, as when plants are too tall or numerous for mechanical control to work. Also employed where a large population of one plant species is being grown, so that a balanced mix of natural predators cannot be expected to develop effective biological control.	Spraying and dusting chemicals are sometimes less precise than other types of control. Impact of the chemical on the user, neighboring plants, animals, and beneficial insects should always be considered. Protect sensitive organisms in the area. Do not equate potential harm with origin of the chemical being applied; pepper spray in the eyes may be as damaging as an oil-based chemical in the lungs.

STAKING

Stake plants before they begin to lean or flop. These grow-through supports were placed above this large globe thistle in early May (left). Within three weeks, the plant hides the supports (right). Because globe thistle is so large, one grow-through is not enough. Interlocking grow-throughs improve their stability.

Grow-through stakes can be gridded (left) or open, like tomato cages (center). Place grow-through supports over the perennial. Guide stems through the supports as they grow. The open stakes provide unobtrusive support for plants that flare out from a narrow base. Individual braces (right) support single stems.

Most garden perennials are not the same as their wild counterparts. They've been improved by breeding. However, the improvements often include larger, taller, heavier flowers that can't stand up to the elements without help.

Sometimes the garden setting creates the need for staking plants that are otherwise sturdy. You'll have to stake if in windy locations and where the soil is too lean or too rich for the plant. Staking will correct plants that lean toward the light where sunlight is strongly one-directional, such as on the east or west side of a building.

Very tall, large-flowered species, such as delphinium, peony, and foxglove, usually require staking. Others tend to flop only in certain circumstances, such as yarrow in a very rich soil. Predicting the fall may take a season's experience with a plant to learn whether it will need staking or will stand on its own.

Stake a plant in spring while it is still short. Stakes, cages, and other props might look awkward when first placed. If they do draw the eye, don't be concerned. Perennials grow so quickly from midspring to early summer that they rapidly cloak the stakes with foliage.

Don't bother to stake after the plant has fallen. Once a perennial has flopped over or been beaten down by rain or wind, cut the flowers and enjoy them in a vase. Even if the fall didn't break the stems or crease them so they can no longer conduct water to the flowers, nothing looks less natural than a plant picked up and lassoed to a stake.

Place single-stake props at graceful angles rather than straight up and down so that stems appear to spray naturally up and out from a single point (the plant's crown). It can be instructive to place the stakes first and be happy with their arrangement before tying in any stems. Green stakes often but not always blend best. Many gardeners keep several different colors of stakes at hand.

SUPPORT, DON'T STRANGLE

Pictured on this page are many types of stakes for perennials. Note that all allow the stem to move. Even stems that grow through a support grid can still sway. Motion is important in plant growth. Cell walls become stronger when the stems are occasionally rocked by wind. When you tie a stem to a stake, tie the twine in a figure eight. That tethers the plant but doesn't prevent motion.

Tight ties can also cut off the vital flow of water; a constricted stem may die before being able to bloom. Use wide, straplike ties rather than thin, stringy material to tie stems; the latter is likely to pinch or snap the stem it binds. Use the soft, natural-colored hemp or

Twiggy branch stakes make natural fences around floppy perennials.

Stake a perennial if it has very heavy flowers (left), if it has fragile stems and is in a windy site (center), or if it grows where light is so strongly one-sided that its flowering stems reach for the sun (right).

green Velcro straps sold at garden centers. Avoid wire, coated-wire twist ties, and fishing line. Don't be stingy—use several ties per stem to distribute the weight.

NO-STAKE STAKING

One alternative to using stakes is to grow unsteady plants next to sturdy ones. The stems of one can lean on the other in an effect called weaving. The look is often a little unusual, but the chance that it might be breathtaking leads most gardeners to experiment.

Another option to staking is to pinch plants, which promotes shorter stems and a bushier habit less likely to tumble. The term pinch might mislead you—it can mean nipping off soft stem tips between thumb and forefinger, but more often it means cutting back stems with sharp shears. Many gardeners are familiar with pinching in relation to chrysanthemums but haven't realized how many other perennials can be clipped back several times between early May and their bloom time to achieve the same effect. The "Plant Gallery" notes whether a perennial is pinchable.

Pinch stems one or more times during spring or early summer. Pinched plants may stand without staking because they are sturdier and shorter. Pinching also delays flowering.

SOME FAMOUS LEANERS AND STURDY NEIGHBORS

Good plant combinations for no-stake staking:
- Jupiter's beard, masterwort, salvia, and bugbane (above)
- Delphinium and hollyhock
- Meadow rue and maiden grass
- Monkshood and goatsbeard
- Aster and feather reed grass
- Tall perennial geraniums and false indigo
- Blazing star and false sunflower

DEADHEADING AND CUTTING BACK

Many perennials, such as this yellow-flowered threadleaf coreopsis, bloom abundantly on thick, bushy plants. Deadheading individual stems is extremely time-consuming. Luckily, these plants respond well to shearing. Catmint, evening primrose, and lavender are others you can treat in the same manner.

Cutting off bloomed-out stalks can stretch a plant's bloom time because it manipulates nature's floral insurance policy. On the stems or crowns of most perennials are buds that can but don't always develop into flowers or flower stalks. If the plant's first flush of bloom is adequately pollinated and sets plentiful seed, the ripening seeds produce hormones that tell the dormant buds they aren't needed.

Deadheading—removing blooms as petals fade but before seed begins to ripen—frees those second-wave flower buds to grow. A perennial might double or triple its bloom time when deadheaded.

Use scissors, clippers, shears or trimmers to remove spent blooms. Just aim to send all or most of a plant's ripening seedpods to the ground. Hedge shears, string trimmers, and even mowers are all effective deadheading tools. Some quick-cut tools may leave a plant with more rough edges than one cut stem by stem with scissors, but new growth soon covers up the cuts.

Removing brown, spent petals and stems gives the garden a fresh look. This chore also eliminates old tissue where some diseases can establish a foothold on otherwise healthy plants.

Yet there are times when deadheading is not desirable—for example, when a perennial has attractive seedpods; bear's breeches and red baneberry are two examples. Others, such as purple coneflower, produce seeds that attract songbirds to the garden. You may not mind the brown of ripening seedpods if they lend interest to the fall or winter scene or bring bright yellow goldfinches and perky chickadees to your garden.

Another type of pruning is done to please the eye. What you do is lop off both leaf and flower to stimulate production of new stems and leaves. This more drastic type of trimming is called cutting back or cutting back hard. It removes much or all of a plant's foliage in one step. Cut back when a perennial's flower production has fallen off for the season. As each stalk blooms out, cut it to the ground or to a point where new growth is evident.

Cutting back hard takes all the stalks at once, removing most or all of the plant's foliage in one day. This is done most often to perennials that grow quickly, bloom before

Fast-growing, early-blooming perennials that become ragged or brown by July are candidates for cutting back hard. That means to prune them all the way back to the ground. Keep the plants well watered until new growth has developed. A large perennial clump can be cut back hard in sections (left) to reduce the size of the temporary hole this leaves in a garden—the east half of the clump might be cut first, followed by the west half seven to 10 days later.

Veronica—standard spike

Blazing star—top-down spike

Coreopsis—ascending bloom

Anemone—descending bloom

Daylily—tip cluster

Bellflower—multicluster

summer's heat, or tend to cease vegetative growth once seeds begin to ripen.
It eliminates tired foliage and encourages the plant to replace it with fresh green leaves, which makes the whole plant look better.

Cutting back hard is a shock to a plant, so take care which perennials you do this to. Spare newly planted or stressed perennials. For instance, though the "Plant Gallery" lists coreopsis as a candidate for cutting back hard,

stick with simple deadheading if your plant suffered deer browsing or severe insect damage, or you transplanted it this season.

Pamper cut-back perennials to support new growth. Give them plentiful water after cutting. Once new growth appears, sidedress the plants with 1 to 2 tablespoons of a balanced liquid fertilizer, such as 20-20-20 dissolved in water.

Perennials with branched flower stalks: Remove single blooms as they fade. New flowers develop further up the stalk on thin stems. Cut back the entire stalk when these stems are too lanky.

DEADHEADING AND CUTTING BACK
continued

DEADHEAD FOR LONG-BLOOMING PERENNIALS

Plant Name	When to Deadhead	Notes
Anise hyssop	Late summer	Cut when flower stalk that has already bloomed is longer than the part with developing flower buds. For later blooms and stronger stems, deadhead earlier and lower on plant.
Bee balm	Midsummer	Remove flowers as they age. Youngest have petals at center, top of disk; oldest flowers, around outer edge of disk.
Bellflower	Early to midsummer	Clip individual flowers plus stems as they fade, then remove entire spike or cluster when last buds have opened.
Blanket flower	Mid- to late summer	Remove whole flower and its stem. Cut back entire stalk when flower stems become too thin and flowers too small.
Blue flax	Early to midsummer	Clip flower stalk to above a leaf when length of stalk that has already bloomed exceeds portion still developing flower buds (produced at tips above seedpods).
Checkerbloom	Mid- to late summer	New flowers are produced at tip of stalk. Remove entire spike when more than half its length has bloomed.
Coral bells	Early to midsummer	Cut off entire flowering stalk at its base when more of its length has bloomed than is developing bloom.
Daisy	Mid- to late summer	Remove whole flower and its stem as center of flower disk turns gold. Cut back entire stalk when flower stems become too thin and flowers too small.
Delphinium	Mid- to late summer	For sturdiest stems on second bloom, cut spike to just above a healthy leaf. Cut entire flower stalk down to basal foliage when flower production slows.
Globe thistle	Mid- to late summer	Remove whole flower and its stem. Cut flower stalk to ground when bud production on that stalk slows.
Golden marguerite	Mid- to late summer	Remove whole flower and its stem. Cut back entire stalk when flower stems become too thin and flowers too small.
Jacob's ladder	Late spring to early summer	Cut when each stalk reaches point where more than half its length has already bloomed. Cut entire stalk to ground when its flower production slows.
Lanceleaf coreopsis	Early to late summer	Remove whole flower and its stem. Cut back entire stalk when flower stems become too thin and flowers too small.
Many-flowered sunflower	Midsummer to fall	Remove whole flower and its stem. Cut flower stalk to the ground when bud production on that stalk slows.
Obedient plant	Late summer to fall	Cut to just above a healthy leaf when the flower spike has finished blooming along more than half its length.
Perennial bachelor's button	Late spring to early summer	Remove each faded flower and its stem, cutting to just above a healthy leaf. Cut entire flower stalk when flower production slows.
Perennial salvia	Early to midsummer	As flower stalks begin to lean away from vertical, cut all to just above main mass of foliage. New flowering shoots may develop from base of plant or along stems.
Pincushion flower	Mid- to late summer	Remove whole flower and its stem. Cut back entire stalk when flower stems become too thin and flowers too small.
Purple coneflower	Midsummer to fall	Remove whole flower and its stem. Cut back entire stalk when flower stems become too thin and flowers too small.
Speedwell	Mid- to late summer	Cut to just above a healthy leaf when the flower spike has finished blooming along more than half its length.
Tall phlox	Late summer to fall	Remove individual flowers from cluster, or cut whole cluster when more of the outer flowers have faded than central buds.
Yarrow	Mid- to late summer	Remove individual flower and its stem when central floret opens. Cut to just above a sturdy side shoot.

WHERE TO CUT

To deadhead most effectively, study the inflorescence to recognize the order in which buds open. Then remove spent flowers and clip stems to promote the buds that will develop into the largest flowers with the thickest stems. Here are the most common types of flower stem arrangements showing the order in which flowers will form and bloom:

A. First flowers to open
B. Buds that will open later
C. Where new flowers emerge after deadheading

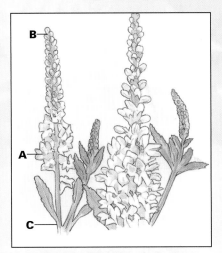

Standard spike: *The tip keeps growing as lower flowers open. Nip individual faded flowers from base of the spike. Eventually, cut off spike when bloomed-out section is longer than portion with buds. Cut lower on the stalk, just above a node, where a leaf joins a stem. Several small stalks develop to replace the one cut. Thin if single-spike appearance desired.*

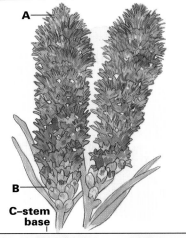

Top-down spike: *Tip flowers open first and bloom proceeds downward. Clip off top of spike as upper flowers fade, or cut entire spike anytime after flower buds on the bottom half open. Additional flower stalks usually develop from leafy part of remaining stem if you cut off the first spike before the lowest buds open.*

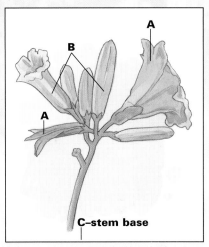

Tip clusters and Heads: *Flowers clustered on a single leafless or nearly leafless stem open one by one. Remove each blossom as it fades or the whole stalk as the last flower finishes blooming. Any subsequent bloom will sprout from the base of the plant. Heads are similar, however, the blossoms are tightly packed. Remove the whole stalk after the last flower fades.*

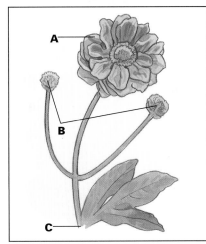

Branched flower stems, descending bloom: *The central, tallest flower opens first. Remove each flower and its stalk as it fades, cutting just above a side branch that has yet to bloom.*

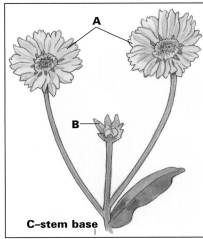

Branched flower stems, ascending bloom: *Flowers on the lowest branches open first. Remove each flower as it fades and clip to main stalk. Cut back stalk completely when it's ungainly.*

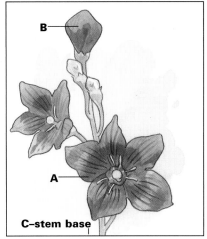

Multicluster flowers: *Open flowers appear all along the stalk, but the flowers in each cluster bloom one by one. Cut the whole stalk down to leafy growth when the last flower blooms.*

DIVIDING

Even with all the cutting you do to keep perennials neat and blooming longer, they'll still produce enough energy to store for next year. This season's nine-stem bee balm may make its debut next spring with 25 stems. The following year the number may run to three figures. Species that multiply rapidly, such as obedient plant and certain artemisias, will overrun less aggressive neighbors. Step in periodically to reduce the size of these overachievers.

Unchecked growth takes a toll. In clump-forming species, such as coral bells and daylilies, many stems growing where once there was just one means there's more competition for nutrients and water. Leaves and flowers become smaller. The plant doesn't rebound as fast from problems or cutting back.

Diseases and insects thrive among weakened tissues and find shelter in crowded stems. Pests, such as powdery mildew on phlox and four-lined plant bug on pincushion flower, can multiply in close, dark spaces and take refuge there in the off-season. The longer a perennial grows without division, the more likely it is to succumb to pest problems.

Some perennials get into trouble quickly and should be divided every two to three years. Others can stay in place for five to six years with little or no loss in health or looks. A few need division so rarely that they are considered permanent plants.

Personal preference also affects frequency of division. Some gardeners divide a plant right after it has impressed them with its mature beauty, figuring it's all downhill after the peak. Others know that a plant will gradually decline in vigor or bloom count; they wait to divide until these effects are noticeable.

DIVIDE IN SPRING AND FALL

Divide perennials in spring or fall when plants reestablish quickly. Cool air and warm soil results in more root than shoot growth. Spring and fall often bring more reliable rains and less evaporation. Soil stays more evenly moist and thus more conducive to root growth, with less follow-up watering to do.

If your schedule allows, divide spring-blooming perennials in fall and fall bloomers in spring. This allows each plant the longest possible time to reestablish itself between division and next bloom.

Sometimes you can't divide when you "should." For example, you may need to renovate a bed that contains both spring-blooming species and fall bloomers. Go ahead

Offsets: *Some perennials expand by forming offsets—or daughter plants—connected "at the hip" to the mother plant. Snap or slice through these connections to obtain pieces with three to seven eyes.*

Eyes: *Multiple eyes or buds form each year at the base of the previous season's stems or on rhizomes or tubers. Each bud will be a new stem and eventually form its own set of roots. Slice cleanly anywhere between the eyes to produce divisions with their own eyes and roots. Even the smallest of these divisions will grow, but those with three to seven eyes are best for replanting.*

Running: *A perennial's roots may run at or below the soil surface and produce new plants at a distance from the mother plant. Or its stems may grow along the surface, forming daughter plants. Each can be cut away to become an independent plant.*

Forked taproot: *Some perennials form one or a few main roots that grow vertical taproots. If a taproot forks below the soil surface to form multiple crowns, that root can be split lengthwise to yield pieces that each have a crown, a portion of taproot, and branching roots or root buds.*

Taproot, single crown: *Not all taproots form multiple crowns. To obtain divisions from them, slice off eyes with some root or cut off pencil-thick side roots. Plant them at an angle just below grade. These will grow as separate plants.*

and dig; then give the plants a little extra aftercare. Stake any divisions that will bloom shortly after being replanted. If it's spring, refrain from cutting back hard because that reduces leaf surface and energy levels before roots can rebuild starch reserves. If it's summer, give extra attention to follow-up watering, and set up screens to block drying winds and midday sun for a week or two.

LIFT OUT PLANTS, CUT ROOTS

To get started, dig or lift out the plant. Use a garden fork to loosen soil all around the plant. Put your fork under it and work the handle like a lever. The perennial will pop out.

Don't hesitate to cut roots. When a perennial needs dividing most, it's not unusual to reduce its root mass and stem count by three-quarters.

If you are unfamiliar with a perennial you are dividing, shake or rinse most of the soil off the roots so its configuration is apparent. You may grow thousands of perennial species in your life but you need to know only about five rooting patterns (see page 40). Once the root pattern is evident, it's usually clear how to proceed.

KEEP YOUNG PLANT PARTS

The youngest parts of a plant, usually the outside edges of a clump, are the healthiest and most vigorous. They have had the least exposure to pests, and they've received the best nutrition—from nutrients outside the main root ball in soil not yet exhausted by older plant parts.

Divide to obtain young pieces. Discard the central, oldest parts. Clip off frayed and injured roots, which can slow reestablishment. Remove all weed roots that have infiltrated the perennial's root ball.

Before replanting divisions, renew the soil to replace nutrients and organic matter. If the perennials you lifted fill a wheelbarrow, mix at least one wheelbarrow of compost or peat-topsoil mix into that spot before replanting. This prevents transplants from settling into unsightly depressions as well as rebuilding the soil's nutrient bank. Divisions that sink below grade are less likely to benefit from airflow around stems and more likely to suffer from excess or standing water.

EXPERIENCE ELIMINATES STEPS IN DIVIDING

Once you know what type of roots there are on a given species, it's possible to skip steps in dividing. The following procedure lets you obtain divisions or reduce a perennial's size without disturbing the entire clump. Always add compost or peat-topsoil mix around the mother clump in a volume equal to the roots and soil removed.

One or more pie-shaped wedges can be removed from a plant that forms offsets, such as hosta. Slice to or beyond the plant's center so that you remove not only outer growth but part of the central, oldest portion.

When perennials produce shoots from shallow runners or stems that recline and develop their own roots, you can cut new shoots from the parent plant and transplant them to a new location.

Where new shoots arise from deeper-running roots, it's possible to loosen and excavate next to the mother plant, then reach below to snap off or cut away a section of root and shoot.

SEASONAL CHORES

When seasons change, perennial gardens change. Perennial gardeners learn to take a few extra steps to see the plants safely through the off-season and give them the very best start every spring.

END-OF-SEASON CUTS

In autumn, when nighttime temperatures drop to near or below freezing and leaves begin to fall from deciduous trees and shrubs, pull out the pruners and shears. Cut back herbaceous perennials that are going dormant and falling down, such as peony and bleeding heart. Shear them to just above ground level.

Removing all of a herbaceous plant's foliage in fall will not harm the plant, even if it is still green when you begin work. Buds for next year are already set at the base of the stems or just below ground level. Cutting removes some of the clutter from a garden, making all other fall tasks easier to complete.

Pass by perennials such as lavender, sage, Russian sage, and thyme, that set next year's growth buds above ground on woody branches. Woody perennials winter best if left intact until early spring. Plants that are not woody but have attractive evergreen foliage, such as Lenten rose and coral bells, can also be left intact over winter.

Hold off cutting perennials with persistent herbaceous stems—black-eyed Susan, 'Autumn Joy' sedum, and ornamental grasses that are not usually knocked down by snow. Now step back to think about how this scene will look from fall until spring. Cut back the ones that do not aesthetically enhance the cold-weather landscape.

Rake or bundle your cuttings. Put them on a compost pile or shred them and use them as mulch.

FALL CLEANUP

PREVENT DISEASE AND PESTS: In the case of plants that had significant disease or insect problems this year or are highly susceptible to pests, be very thorough in cutting and cleaning up these plants, and take precautions when disposing of the waste. Don't shred these plants for mulch. Their foliage, stems, and leaf litter may hold fungus spores, bacterial resting bodies, or insect eggs that should be removed from the area.

One way to dispose of infected or suspect debris is to compost it in a pile kept *hot* by regular turning. The heat of active decomposition kills most diseases and insects. You can also bury the debris at least 18 inches deep or burn it.

APPLY SLOW-RELEASE FERTILIZER: After cutting and raking away debris, save time on next year's work by applying a slow-release fertilizer such as 8-6-8 bulb food or 6-2-0 Milorganite. Spread ¼ to ½ cup for every 10 square feet. This material will become mixed into the soil and covered during the next steps in fall cleanup. It will degrade gradually so that by spring its nutrients will be available to perennials during their first flush of growth.

WEED THOROUGHLY: Remove all weeds that were hiding under the skirts of perennials. Loosen and remove persistent perennial weeds, lifting perennials if necessary to trace and eliminate all weed roots.

Recut trenched edges. Leave the trench open and free of mulch during winter—an air barrier effectively deters root growth.

If the bed is encircled by a root barrier, check for and grub out running weeds that may have slipped under, over, or in between sections of edging. Repair and re-anchor edging as necessary.

DIVIDE, PLANT, ADD BULBS: Divide spring-blooming perennials that need renewal or restraint. It's also a good time to dig out and discard perennials that have not performed up to expectations, and replace them with species better suited to the site and your needs. While you're making design changes, consider adding spring-blooming hardy bulbs around and even beneath late-emerging species, such as hibiscus and Japanese anemone.

RENEW MULCH: Now add mulch around the crowns and between perennials, bringing

Cut back herbaceous perennials that form buds at or below the ground, like these plants, in fall.

Wait until spring to cut shrubby perennials that set buds on woody branches (Russian sage).

this blanket up to the desired depth: 1 to 2 inches of woody material or bark, 2 to 3 inches of leafy matter, pods, or hulls. Use the abundance of tree leaves, which can be shredded or used whole, as mulch. Avoid using black walnut leaves, which break down into compounds that can stunt or kill some perennials. Mix very large, decay-resistant leaves, such as sycamore, oak, and Norway maple, with smaller leaves to prevent formation of dense mats. Or mow or shred such leaves before applying.

SPECIAL PROTECTION FOR A FEW:
Every perennial gardener sooner or later tries to push the hardiness of a plant. If you're growing a few marginally hardy perennials—species not known to be reliably hardy in your hardiness zone—applying 12 to 18 inches of loose, airy mulch over the crown and root zone may give the plants enough protection to survive the winter. A mound of straw covered with evergreen boughs held down by a length of wire-mesh fencing works well.

This protection may prevent damage to perennials that are planted very late—when less than three to four weeks remain before frost is likely to enter the soil. Water the plants well, being sure to moisten the soil all around the root ball, before applying the mulch.

Finally, clean up your tools and put away the wheelbarrow and hoses for the winter. It's going to be a wonderful, easy spring because your perennial garden is so well prepared.

SPRING START-UP

When the foliage of the earliest bulbs emerges in your yard, cut down and dispose of the perennial stems you left standing for winter interest. Remove any protective mulches from marginally hardy and late-planted perennials, and check the beds for any crusted or matted mulch that may slow perennial reemergence. You don't have to remove the mulch; just break up the mats.

Give summer-blooming woody perennials a haircut to promote dense growth. Cut the stems of lavender, Russian sage, thyme, Montauk daisy, and artemisia so that only a few healthy buds remain at the base of each branch. Steel yourself—although it seems drastic, this cutting promotes dense growth very quickly.

You might choose to cut back some evergreen foliage now. Taking away Lenten rose's winter-tattered

Perennial gardens can look good all year. In fall, cut back selectively to create a winterscape of well-placed plants with sturdy stems and attractive forms.

leaves can make its early-spring show that much prettier, and cutting away old coral bells foliage showcases emerging greenery.

Fertilize perennials as they emerge, if you didn't apply the slow-release fertilizer in fall.

Weed thoroughly; there are always a few weeds that escaped notice in fall, usually under or behind those perennials you left standing for winter interest. Top up mulch as necessary to deny any weed seeds a place in the sun.

Then sit back and enjoy the show. You are well ahead of the game this year!

SPARE THE BUDS

Cut back hard woody perennials like lavender in early spring. Remove spent foliage and trim remaining stems nearly to the ground (see plants at the sides of the photo).

Within three weeks, the plants will be growing strong and be cleaner and neater-looking, unlike the untrimmed lavender in the center of the photo.

TROUBLESHOOTING

Groundhogs often knock down large plants to reach the flower buds and succulent tips they prefer.

This chapter will help you identify specific culprits and choose a control strategy when plant damage is serious enough to warrant your intervention.

RABBITS: They nibble foliage and neatly snip off individual stems and leaves of many perennials. Damage is often heaviest early in the year. Favorite plants include aster, balloon flower, bellflowers, hosta, pincushion flower, pinks, and purple coneflower.

■ **Control strategies:** For small plants, floating row cover—lightweight material that allows light and water to pass through—bars their feeding. Keep plants covered until they are well-established and can tolerate some browsing. Fence whole beds or cage large plants individually. Use wire with ½-inch mesh, such as rabbit hutch wire. Make fences 18 to 24 inches tall. (Dark green or black fencing is nearly invisible at a distance for whole-bed fencing. Cages around individual plants are visible in spring when the plants most need protection, but are usually hidden by plant growth within weeks.) Where rabbits are numerous, they may resort to digging; bend the wire to make an 8-inch L at the bottom of the fence. Bury the L under mulch, facing out (see the illustration on page 45).

Capture and relocate the rabbits. Use fresh greens to bait traps, and set them early in the season when other food is scarce. Check local ordinances regulating relocation.

Repellents such as distasteful sprays or scented items may be temporarily effective. Individual rabbits differ in reaction, so change products often, from thiram-based spray to hot pepper wax or blood meal, for example.

Set up scarecrows, such as toy animals with large eyes, near favored plants; move them often. Motion-activated electronic devices startle pests with water sprays or sound.

GROUNDHOGS, GOPHERS, AND PRAIRIE DOGS: These vegetarians are great diggers; groundhogs (or woodchucks) climb as well. Groundhogs prefer shoots, flower buds, and fruit. Prairie dogs and gophers eat roots. This group has diverse tastes, including bellflowers, checkerbloom, daylilies, delphinium, and phlox.

■ **Control strategies:** Capture and relocate; use tactics similar to those used for

Rabbits often work from the bottom toward the top of a plant and may prefer one side of a plant or garden that is closer to shelter. They may leave behind clusters of dark brown pellets.

Emerging perennials, like this hosta, are particularly vulnerable. Rabbits bite cleanly through stems and leaf stalks.

rabbits, such as laying row cover fabric over young plants, or fencing the garden with 1-inch mesh wire (chicken wire). Fence over the beds and all around them. Or make fences 36 inches tall, leaving the top 12 inches unsupported so that an animal climbing the fence will fall outward when reaching that section. These pests are quick to dig, so continue the fence underground with an additional L that extends 12 to 24 inches down and 12 inches outward.

Other strategies: Use repellents or set up scarecrows, as for rabbits.

SQUIRRELS, GROUND SQUIRRELS, AND CHIPMUNKS: These pests cause damage by digging up recently planted perennials. They don't usually eat perennials but may do so if their population is high and other food sources are scarce.

■ **Control strategies:** Capture and relocate the pests. Peanut butter is a reliable bait. Check local ordinances regulating relocation or destruction.

Discourage digging. These critters are most likely to dig where soil has been loosened, such as around new plantings. Cover a freshly planted area with row cover for a few days, weighting the edges of the cloth with logs or planks. To end digging, lay pieces of ½-inch mesh wire fencing on the soil around threatened plants.

Use repellents. Hot pepper wax or blood meal sprayed or spread on the soil may be temporarily effective.

Encourage predators. Cats, hawks, and owls suppress rodents in general.

VOLES: Voles, or "meadow mice," can be especially destructive in winter, devouring bulbs, tubers, and perennial crowns.

Look for clean 1-inch entrance holes, darting motion in beds, and neatly clipped stems or shaved crowns. In cold regions, voles may eat the crowns of lawn grass under cover of snow. When melting snow reveals shallow

furrows cut through a lawn, it's a sure sign that voles have struck.

■ **Control strategies:** Set out mousetraps baited with peanut butter in early spring before the vole population grows. Set traps near entry holes. Cover each trap with an inverted shoebox cut out on one side so that the area is dark but open to the voles. Check traps at least once a day.

Encourage predators, as you would in handling squirrels and rabbits.

BIRDS: Occasionally birds are destructive by feeding on or uprooting seedlings or damaging foliage in pursuit of pests.

■ **Control strategies:** Protect young or special plants. Cover plants with bird netting or row cover, or set up scarecrows.

DEER, ELK, AND MOOSE: They prefer but do not limit their feeding to young growth and flower buds. In winter, they may paw up and crop perennial crowns.

■ **Control strategies:** Exclude grazers. Install electric fencing or barriers at least 8 feet tall (deer). Dark plastic mesh fencing is effective and reasonably priced.

Set up motion-sensitive scarecrows. These startle intruders with water sprays or sound and are effective from spring to fall if repositioned frequently.

Even if you select "deer-resistant" species, the deer may sample or trample them. Fence them until the plants are well-established and able to tolerate occasional abuse.

To thwart digging, form an 8-inch L at the base of a rabbit fence. Cover it with soil or mulch.

Deer eat many perennials and have become so accustomed to people that they cause problems even in city gardens. Fences remain the gardener's best defense against deer.

Each deer herd may have unique tastes, but hostas are so popular that they're dubbed deer candy.

INSECTS, MITES, AND MOLLUSKS

Plant bugs, like most sucking insects, concentrate on soft new foliage and do the most damage to the small young leaves.

Soft-bodied, slow-moving aphids cluster on stem tips, flower buds, and the undersides of young foliage. Aphid feeding can siphon off so much water that flower buds abort and new leaves are stunted or cupped.

Spittlebugs suck juices from stems. Look for them on the stems below growth that is distorted.

Foliage attacked by whiteflies may look similar to that damaged by mites. Surfaces under the feeding site may be shiny or sticky from insect droppings. Check the undersides of the leaf; whitefly nymphs shed exoskeletons there. Look for adults flying from the plant when disturbed.

Mites are too small to be seen by the naked eye, but the distinctive pale, stippled appearance of the foliage will alert you to check for these eight-legged spider relatives. Look at the undersides of leaves with a magnifier.

Small creatures can wreak havoc on a garden. These tips will help you protect your perennials from an array of insects.

SUCKING INSECTS: These include aphids, plant bugs, mites, spittlebugs, thrips, and leafhoppers, all of which suck nutrient-rich liquid from plant cells. Sucking insects are always present and cause little noticeable damage unless the population reaches a certain size. Then you may start to see disfigured plants with pockmarks or pale spots drained of nutrients. These pests prefer young foliage, and their feeding frequently causes the new growth to be stunted, puckered, or twisted. The plant may shed heavily damaged foliage.

■ **Control strategies:** Identify which pest is the problem. If it is mites, begin spraying with miticides, such as fenbutatin-oxide (Orthenex), when damage first becomes noticeable. Insecticidal soap, acephate (Orthene), and carbaryl (Sevin) are effective against many sucking insects. Summer-weight horticultural oil, hot pepper spray, and some insecticidal soaps kill both insects and mites (check the label). Follow label directions.

Dislodge mites, aphids, or nonflying stages of whiteflies and leafhoppers. Hose off foliage, both upper and lower surfaces. Repeat every few days until new damage ceases.

Lacewings, lady beetles, predatory mites, dragonflies, birds, and other "beneficials" keep pest numbers below harmful levels. To promote them, spray to target only specific plants and pests, and grow a wide variety of flowering plants for pollen and shelter sites. You can purchase natural predators and introduce them into the garden.

When leaf edges are paler than veins or the leaf appears to be lightly browned, flip the leaf to look for leafhoppers. They drain much sap from a leaf but also inject a toxin that can cause a pale or toasted color on leaf edges.

Clean up well in fall. To remove eggs and overwintering pests on persistent perennial stalks, eliminate plant debris around infested plants. Compost, burn, or remove this debris.

LEAF- AND FLOWER-CHEWING INSECTS: Sawflies, beetles, earwigs, caterpillars, and leaf miners are among these pests. Some of them eat the leaf but avoid the veins. Others tunnel into and eat only the tissue sandwiched between upper and lower leaf surfaces. Many eat the entire leaf or petal. Insects in this group are recognized by the plant they feed on as well as the pattern of their damage—how, when, and which plant parts they eat.

Plants that lose less than 20 percent of their foliage to chewing insects often don't show significant loss of vigor or bloom. In fact, chewing-insect damage often does not even draw attention until it has become severe. At that point it's usually too late to control the pests because their feeding is finished or near an end for the season. Bide your time and plan to fend off the attack next year. Make a note of the date when you first noticed the damage, then subtract two to three weeks. That's when you need to start checking the plants.

■ **Control strategies:** Destroy the insects as they feed. Sheltered feeders (leaf miners and caterpillars that roll or tie leaves together) are protected from most insecticides but can be controlled by removing and destroying all affected foliage. To kill sheltered feeders with an insecticide, select a product with systemic action, such as acephate (Orthene). Plants absorb systemic insecticides and incorporate them in their tissues. Contact insecticides either temporarily coat the outside of the plant and the pest ingests it as it feeds or kill by directly contacting the insect.

Chewing insects that feed openly (beetles, earwigs, sawflies, and some caterpillars) can be plucked off by hand and destroyed or sprayed with a contact insecticide. Use carbaryl (Sevin), malathion, or insecticidal soap. Young caterpillars can be killed if leaves they eat are dusted with Dipel (Bt, or *Bacillus thuringiensis*), a bacteria affecting moth and butterfly larvae.

Destroy the insects as they lay eggs, or destroy the eggs. Most sawfly, leaf miner, and caterpillar eggs are deposited on the plant two to three weeks before damage reaches noticeable levels.

Check your notes as to when the damage first appeared in previous years. Then, two to three weeks before that date, apply a contact insecticide to kill egg-laying adults. Or wait until after eggs are laid; then spray summer-weight horticultural oil to suffocate the larvae. Protect susceptible plants with floating row cover fabric for a week to 10 days to prevent insects from laying eggs or chewing foliage.

Flowers that open with brown streaks and distortions are probably infested with thrips. They are 1/20 inch long and might be visible at the base of petals.

Sawflies (caterpillar-like larvae of nonstinging wasps) blend with the leaves they eat and clean up the evidence of their presence by shaving leaf edges until they have devoured everything but the leaf stalk. Watch for this damage only on plants susceptible to sawfly damage.

Many beetles eat foliage and flower petals. Most chew holes all the way through a leaf, but some, such as Japanese beetle, are skeletonizers. They cut away a leaf's surface, then eat the tissue beneath, leaving a thin skin between the intact veins. They gradually turn a leaf into a lacy skeleton. Japanese beetles are active during the day.

Leaf miners lay eggs on the host plant's foliage. The eggs hatch and the larvae chew into the leaf and feed there, each one creating a serpentine tunnel within the leaf. Tissue around the "mine" eventually turns brown. A hole at the widest end of the mine indicates the larva has finished feeding and exited.

INSECTS, MITES, AND MOLLUSKS
continued

Clean the garden in fall. To eliminate overwintering eggs or larvae or to expose them to predators and weather, remove and destroy all leaf litter, stems, and mulch from around the infested plant. Cultivate the soil lightly and leave it unmulched over winter. Predators and frost will kill the larvae. Encourage predators as you would for sucking insects.

STEM CUTTERS AND BORERS: Cutworms are caterpillars that chew stalks at their base, cutting off stems near the ground. This can kill seedlings. Larger plants may not be killed, but the injury increases disease risk.

Stalk borers chew into the stem some distance above ground or tunnel down from the tip and feed at the stem's center. Everything above the feeding site is usually killed. Although this may affect only several

Cutworms are moth larvae that hide in the soil or mulch during the day, then coil around and bite off small stems at night or cut holes in leaves.

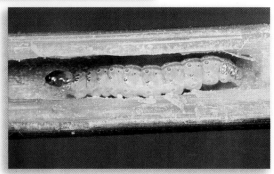

European corn borers sometimes drill into the stems of perennial bachelor's button, delphinium, or aster.

Earwigs are sometimes beneficial, preying on other insect larvae, slugs, and snails. But other times they attack plants. Earwigs' nighttime feeding resembles beetle damage, except earwigs often target flower petals. Suspect earwigs if the damage happens overnight and appears first on flower petals. Confirm it by checking the plants by flashlight at night.

inches of the stem tip, it may also disfigure the plant, often just before it flowers.

To recognize damage by stemcutters, look for seedlings and small stems cut off at the soil line and left lying where they fell. If you cultivate 2 inches deep near the damage, you are likely to unearth rubbery, coiled gray-brown caterpillars—cutworms.

Wilted stem tips are a sign of borers. Cut the damaged stem below the wilted section and split the stem lengthwise to find the grublike moth larva inside.

■ **Control strategies:** For stalk borers, apply a systemic insecticide such as acephate (Orthene). For cutworms, apply carbaryl (Sevin) to the bases of susceptible plants.

Cutworms live in the soil over winter. Cultivate the soil where cutworm damage was heavy, and do not apply new mulch so that birds, other predators, and weather can reach the cutworms. Stalk borers overwinter in perennial stalks, so cut and dispose of or destroy stems of plants with borer damage.

To keep cutworms away from seedlings, circle each seedling with a 3-inch-high cardboard tube to form a collar. Press it into the soil, leaving 2 inches above ground.

Newly hatched stem borers and eggs can be dislodged from perennials with frequent forceful, cool-water drenches over several weeks, beginning when lilacs bloom.

ROOT-FEEDING PESTS: They include weevils (a type of beetle), root aphids, root mealybugs, and nematodes (soil-dwelling, near-microscopic relatives of parasitic roundworms). Perennial roots attacked by these pests are unable to draw sufficient water and nutrients from the soil and may not be able to support or anchor the plant. Plants that wilt before others and show reduced growth may be suffering root damage. To diagnose the problem, dig up suspect plants and examine the roots.

Root weevils feed from fall to spring. Get suspicious if perennial clumps shrink in size over winter, the foliage of evergreen perennials dries out in early spring, or established perennial crowns peel away from their roots.

An absence of new, crisp, light-colored tips on roots and the presence of small white grubs (⅓ inch) on or near the root mass in fall or spring indicates a root weevil infestation. From midsummer into fall, you can identify adult weevil feeding by notched edges on the foliage of the troubled plant or on neighboring plants.

Small grayish-white insects in clusters on the roots may be root aphids or root mealybugs.

Roots stunted and disfigured by nodules indicate nematodes. Some feed in foliage, creating brown areas between main veins. Foliar nematode damage begins with the lowest leaves and spreads upward in hot, damp weather.

■ **Control strategies:** Adult weevils feed on foliage at night from midsummer through fall. Destroy them by spraying the foliage with a systemic insecticide such as acephate beginning in midsummer; follow label directions. Alternatively, go out at night at frequent intervals, beginning in midsummer, and spread a light-colored drop cloth under the infested plant(s). Shake the plants to dislodge the wingless, night-feeding weevils, then gather in the cloth and destroy the weevils you find there. Continue until you no longer shake off any weevils.

Kill weevil grubs in late summer or fall by drenching the soil under infested plants with acephate or another systemic insecticide.

Dip root balls infested with root aphids or mealybugs into a bucket of water containing carbaryl (Sevin). Mix the solution per label directions.

Remove and burn plants with nematode-infested roots. Replace soil that was in contact with the roots of those plants. Replant with a different species. Whenever possible, select replacement varieties that are nematode-resistant, which should be identified in catalogs with an "N" resistance code.

Remove and burn nematode-infested leaves regularly. Also destroy foliage one or two leaves above such damage.

Encourage or introduce natural predators such as beneficial nematodes to attack all root pests. You can purchase them from some mail-order garden suppliers.

SLUGS AND SNAILS: They are mollusks that rasp holes in foliage. Small plants may be destroyed by their feeding. Larger, more established plants are usually only disfigured.

These pests are most common in shady areas and active at night. Inspect damaged plants by flashlight. Slugs are legless, elongated, soft-bodied, and gray, black, or brown. Their eyes are set on stalks protruding from their heads. They range in size from ⅛ inch to several inches. Snails carry a shell covering their body but have the same stalked eyes. Silvery slime trails may be visible near the damage.

■ **Control strategies:** Use bait or granules containing metaldehyde or methiocarb. Scatter the slug-killing product around damaged plants and in nearby shaded, moist areas where the pests may hide during the day. Repeat this process following label directions until new damage is reduced or eliminated. Do not use slug bait around pets or small children.

Inverted, hollowed-out fruit rinds, moist sections of cardboard, or slug traps will capture pests. Check traps daily in late afternoon.

In early spring where slug and snail damage was heavy the previous year, rake away all mulch and debris and dispose of it off-site or in a hot compost pile. This will remove many

Some caterpillars feed in the open, trimming leaf edges evenly or cutting rounded, irregular holes into the leaf. Other caterpillars create shelters in which to feed by folding a leaf to make a pocket or pulling two leaves around themselves and gluing them together with silk. Bits of leaf tissue and insect excrement litter the shelter, making the feeding site quite messy.

Slugs and snails use a rasplike tongue to grate holes in leaves, usually between the veins and within the leaf blade rather than at the margin.

Clumps of perennials that shrink in size over winter, have desiccated foliage, or peel away from the ground for lack of new roots may be infested with root weevils.

Distorted, stunted roots with unnatural nodules are typical of nematode infestation. Roots may be discolored in advanced cases.

overwintering slugs, snails, and eggs. Do not mulch the area until spring rains have tapered off or summer heat has begun. During this time, set out traps. Clean them regularly.

DISEASES

Protect your plants from debilitating diseases. Learn to recognize the symptoms and practice prevention.

LEAF SPOT, RUST, AND SCORCH: These are some of the most common fungal and bacterial infections that disfigure perennials. Spots are distinct when they first appear but may merge over time to form large, irregular dead areas. Rusts are fungal spots that are reddish-brown and raised. Scorch appears as dead leaf margins.

Although spots, rusty marks, and burnt leaf edges may occur without any connection to disease, it's wise to investigate further when they appear. Read more about the affected plant so you can rule out causes such as genetics; some plant species develop natural spots or streaks as leaves age. Also take a critical look at the environment and the plant's recent care; leaves can scorch or discolor under adverse conditions, such as heat, drought, and overfertilization.

In addition, it's important to know whether you face a disease or insect because control strategies aimed at one will usually have no effect on the other. To distinguish between the two, look closely at spots and dead leaf margins. A hand lens helps. If a blemish is caused by disease, leaf tissue is generally intact while an insect's chewing creates a hole or scrape marks. However, the center of older diseased spots may dry up and fall out.

Dead areas caused by disease often have concentric rings or expand in bands that are pale green where the infection is still spreading; yellow in tissue that has been infected a bit longer; and brown or black at the points that were first infected.

Advanced stages of an infection are often very distinctive, with marks caused by a particular disease having a certain shape, margin, or color. Reference books often describe only these advanced symptoms. Once you know to watch for a problem, you should be able to catch it earlier—when infected areas simply appear paler than surrounding tissue or look water-soaked. These early signs are more visible if you hold the leaf up and look through it toward a light source.

Infection often starts on lower, older foliage and in the interior of the plant—wherever there is less light or air movement or more moisture and stress. Later, it spreads higher on the plant as spores from the first spots move up with splashing water.

■ **Control strategies:** Even when many leaves are disfigured, most perennials can still produce enough energy to address day-to-day needs and come back bigger the next season. Your main concern should be arresting the infection's spread so it will not recur.

Remove debris around infected and susceptible plants. Check often for infected leaves and remove them immediately. Cut down and remove herbaceous stems at the end of the season. Burn potentially infectious material or throw it away. Dispose of it in a compost pile only if you regularly turn the pile to keep it heated to 140° F. Wash your hands and tools after working with infected plants. Often, this is the only control needed to keep these diseases in check.

Select plants carefully. If you learn that a perennial you have or plan to buy is susceptible to these diseases, consider alternative species or try to purchase disease-resistant varieties.

Manage susceptible plants to reduce infection. Grow plants in the recommended amount of sun, keep them well-watered, provide a well-drained bed, and don't over- or underfertilize. Thin out the plants every year, spacing clumps farther apart and watering only in the morning. These tactics make the area unfriendly to fungi because drying air circulates freely between widely spaced stems and wet foliage dries quickest at midday.

Apply preventive fungicides to particularly susceptible plants. Fungicides protect

Leaf spot on bellflower may signal botrytis, an aggravating fungal infection because it infects and kills barely developed flower buds in early spring.

uninfected tissue and may reduce the contagiousness of existing infection. They cannot repair damaged areas.

Begin spraying several weeks before your pest patrol experience tells you that symptoms of the disease may appear. Three to six fungicide applications are generally necessary, at intervals stipulated on the fungicide label.

Use two or more fungicides. Alternate their use during a season and from year to year to reduce the chance that the fungus or bacteria will become resistant to these products. When alternating fungicides, make the first few applications with one product, then switch to one based on a different active ingredient. For instance, alternate between a sulfur-based fungicide and one containing captan, chlorothalonil (Daconil), copper, ferbam, horticultural oil (Volck), sodium bicarbonate (as in baking soda solutions), or triforine (Funginex). Read the product package to be sure it is labeled for the particular problem and the plant.

MILDEW: Powdery and downy mildews are fungal diseases of leaves, flowers, and stems. They are named for the white or fuzzy appearance they give to foliage when the infection reaches an advanced stage. Mildews are not usually life-threatening, especially to established perennials, but they can be unsightly.

Mildew proliferates where relative humidity is high. It does not develop in high heat, direct sunlight, or on continuously wet leaf surfaces. Monitor susceptible plants for this disease in spring and again in late summer when the day's warmth fades rapidly in the evening and relative humidity is high.

The characteristic powder or fuzz that may appear on the top or bottom of a leaf, stem, or flower is the final stage of the disease. However, foliage is sometimes infected so rapidly when conditions are right that leaves yellow, curl, and die before the telltale mildew can form. Plant parts that are mildewed or yellowed and curled can't be saved, although the plant may generate new foliage if you take action to arrest the infection.

It's more effective to watch for the early signs of infection. At that first stage, a leaf or stem develops pale blotches—areas where developing fungi are destroying the green chlorophyll within the tissues. Infection is most likely to start on the youngest foliage during the spring infection cycle and on lower, inner, or shaded foliage later in the year.

■ **Control strategies:** Clean up. Remove all plant debris from around infected and susceptible plants as you do for leaf spot.

Select and tend plants carefully. Where environmental conditions are right for the

Mildew is rarely life-threatening but often disfiguring. Although you may not see the telltale powdery appearance of leaves until late summer, control is by prevention earlier in the season.

development of mildew, be sure to select mildew-resistant species and varieties. (See "Plant Gallery.") Manage susceptible plants to reduce infection, as explained for leaf spot, rust, and scorch.

Apply preventive fungicides, as with leaf spots, rust, and scorch.

CANKERS: Cankers are infections of the stem and are often caused by the same disease organisms responsible for leaf spot. But the damage caused may be far greater than that caused by leaf spot because the canker may spread down into the roots to kill the plant or sideways to kill the whole stem.

Look for sunken or discolored spots on stalks or elongated wounds like parted lips on the stems of woody evergreens.

Root and crown rot are most often connected with poorly drained soil. If you suspect it, look for soft, rotted black or brown sections at the base of the plant's stems or on the roots.

DISEASES
continued

■ **Control strategies:** Clean up well where cankers are seen. Prune to remove the infected parts. Dip pruning tools in bleach to disinfect. Control leaf spot and other leaf diseases on the plant, to reduce the sources of infection.

ROOT AND CROWN ROT: Root and crown rot are infections of the root and the dormant buds and stem bases of the perennial crown. They are often secondary infections, invading a plant after it has been damaged by excess or insufficient watering, freezing, or excessive fertilizer.

These diseases are most often connected with poorly drained soil. In such areas, look for stunted plants, aborted flower buds, dead leaf tips, or foliage that wilts, then turns yellow or red and dies. If you suspect root and crown rot, examine those plants for soft, rotted black or brown sections at the base of their stems or on their roots. Rotted sections may have a foul odor. The outer covering of a root that's rotted may easily slide off its stringy core.

Symptoms may suddenly appear on the first warm spring days. That's when fungi that invaded roots or buds damaged by freezing, standing water, or drought during the winter begin to proliferate. Sometimes, though, the infection may not be noticeable until winter is long past. This can happen when growing

conditions are perfect for that plant during the season after the damage. As much as 20 percent of a root system may be infected, yet there may be no symptoms because the remainder of the plant is able to overgrow the weak parts. Unfortunately, such a plant may collapse quickly as soon as heat, drought, or other stresses appear.

■ **Control strategies:** Improve growing conditions to support the plant and suppress the diseases. Let the soil dry out between waterings and improve drainage. Make sure plants are growing in the correct amount of light. Don't overfertilize. Avoid overcrowding plants. Ensure strong root systems by dividing perennials regularly.

Root and crown rot diseases don't thrive in biologically active soil. Where you have seen or suspected crown or root rot, mix compost or mycorrhizal innoculants such as MycoRise, MycorTree, or Plant Success into the soil. Then replant the space.

Handle infected plants carefully. Always discard old, weak parts when dividing perennials. If a weak plant shows signs of root or crown rot, dig it up. If it's heavily infected, discard it and the soil around its roots. For those with less rot, cut out diseased portions. Dip the remaining healthy divisions in fungicide. Replant them where the growing conditions are better. Disinfect tools used around the plants with bleach.

BLIGHTS AND WILTS: Blights and wilts are fungal and bacterial infections that enter plants through injuries, roots, or pores on leaves. They then proliferate and clog the water-conducting system.

Investigate stems or plants that wilt suddenly and do not recover after watering. Look for physical damage to stem bases, drainage problems, or root-grazing insects, any of which can cause similar symptoms. If you don't find any of these other causes, suspect wilt or blight. To further differentiate wilts and blights from other problems, cut off a wilted and a healthy stem. Wilts and blights may discolor tissues inside the stem, which you can see by comparing the ends of these cut stems.

Early symptoms of wilt and blight are subtle. Leaves may yellow, or they may wilt and die. Individual leaves, the foliage on one side of the plant, or just the older, lower leaves may be affected. Usually these leaves

Stem canker infections can be more serious problems than leaf infections. A canker may spread on the stem or into the roots to kill whole stems or plants.

remain attached to the plant even after dying. Keep an eye on related plants near a perennial that dies of wilt. The disease may spread to them.

■ **Control strategies:** Clean up around infected and susceptible plants. Immediately remove infected plants and the soil around their roots. Burn or throw out this infectious material. Dispose of it in a compost pile only if you turn the compost regularly to keep it heated to 140° F. Wash your hands and dip tools in bleach or rubbing alcohol after working with infected plants.

Select and tend plants carefully. If you learn that a particular perennial you plan to buy is prone to blight or wilt, or if an existing perennial exhibits susceptibility, consider alternative species or disease-resistant varieties. Wilt- and blight-resistant plants may be identified by a "V" or "F" in catalogs, for resistance to two of the most common wilt pathogens, verticillium and fusarium.

Keep susceptible plants strong to reduce risk of infection. Divide plants regularly and discard the oldest, weakest parts. Locate plants where they receive the right amount of sun. Keep them watered, improve drainage in the bed, and avoid over- or underfertilizing. A well-sited, well-tended perennial resists infection better than a plant weakened by adverse conditions.

VIRUSES: Mosaic, ring spot, and other viruses weaken plants. They are most often spread by insects such as leafhoppers, beetles, and aphids. The insects feed on infected plants, then move to healthy plants where their feeding injects the virus.

Reduced growth may be the first symptom of a virus, followed by stunting, irregular growth, and discoloration of leaves and flowers. Flowers may have light or dark streaks in them. Blooming may decrease or stop. Leaves may be curled or have cupped edges, blotches, streaks, or patterns of yellow or white. The discolored tissues often do not die and may be mistaken for variegation.

■ **Control strategies:** Select plants carefully. Reject plants with viral symptoms. If you know a species is susceptible to a particular virus, select a variety that has proven to be resistant. For instance, a "T" in some catalog descriptions and on plant tags means the variety is resistant to tobacco mosaic virus.

Remove infected plants immediately. Viruses are not transmitted through soil, so soil removal is not necessary. Control the carriers of the virus. Insects are most often the vectors that carry viruses between plants; the most likely culprits are leafhoppers and beetles, which move freely among plants. Aphids are also known to ingest a virus from

one plant then inject it into another. Keep leaf-sucking and leaf-chewing insect populations under control to reduce the spread of viruses. (See control strategies under the various insect groups.)

Insects may transmit viruses to perennials from nearby related weeds, so keep weeds under control as well.

Investigate plants that wilt suddenly and do not recover after watering. If you find no physical damage, drainage problems, or root-grazing insects, suspect blight.

Viruses weaken plants. The first symptom may be reduced growth, followed by stunting, irregular growth, and discoloration of leaves and flowers. Viruses are most often spread by insects such as leafhoppers, beetles, and aphids.

WEEDS: A ROGUE'S GALLERY

Cool-season annuals such as rocket rob perennials of nutrients and space by germinating in late fall or late winter.

Purslane fools us by waiting to sprout until we think the spring weeding is done.

Burdock's large leaves are impressive.

Here are some of the most common and worst weeds of perennial beds. Each weed pictured here represents a group of weeds with the same life cycle—annual, biennial, or perennial—and manner of spread. Effective ways to eradicate the weeds in each group are given. If a weed you seek isn't listed specifically, simply find the group into which it fits to learn some appropriate control tactics.

COOL-SEASON ANNUALS

REPRESENTATIVE: Tall rocket or wild mustard. Seeds germinate in cool weather, late fall, or late winter. Plants are usually large enough to be in flower by the time gardeners begin weeding beds in spring. That means the weeds use up nutrients that could have fueled the perennial bed's resurgence, slow down emerging perennials with their shade, and add another crop of weed seeds to the soil.
CONTROL: Weed thoroughly in fall and apply a seed-smothering mulch or preemergence herbicide to all bare ground. Follow up in early spring as daffodil foliage emerges—remove any cool-season weeds that sprouted in the shallow mulch next to perennial crowns.
OTHER WEEDS IN THIS GROUP: Creeping speedwell, henbit, mouse-ear chickweed, annual bluegrass.

WARM-SEASON ANNUALS

REPRESENTATIVE: Purslane. Seedlings are an indicator of warm soil. They germinate in mid- to late spring as soil temperatures reach 60° F. A sun lover, purslane is most prevalent at the front of a border and between stepping-stones. Because detached, rootless bits of its succulent stems can survive even high heat and generate new roots, it should not be hoed but pulled.
CONTROL: Mulch all bare spaces or apply a preemergence herbicide by midspring. Follow up in early summer and remove any plants that prevailed before they begin to flower. If you fail to take steps early, use mulch to smother the seedlings while they are still tiny.
OTHER WEEDS IN THIS GROUP: Crabgrass, knotweed, ragweed, redroot pigweed, spurge, wild buckwheat, annual wild morning glory (also called bindweed or hedge bindweed).

BIENNIALS

REPRESENTATIVE: Burdock. This is an impressive weed. Its large, felty leaves can dwarf even the largest hosta. Like most biennials, it is a low rosette of foliage with a taproot in its first year. In its second year, it forms a tall flowering stalk. The flowers are unremarkable, but its grape-sized, super-sticky burrs are unmistakable.
CONTROL: Pull, cut, or apply a nonspecific systemic herbicide such as glyphosate (Roundup) before these weeds flower and set seed. Then keep the area well mulched to prevent existing seed in the soil from sprouting.
OTHER WEEDS IN THIS GROUP: Bull thistle, motherwort, mullein, Queen Anne's lace.

CLUMP-FORMING PERENNIALS

REPRESENTATIVE: Dandelion. This and other clump-forming weeds have one quality that works in the gardener's favor—they stay in one place rather than reaching out with their roots to form colonies. Because dandelion roots are deep, the soil has to be loosened deeply to remove the whole root, or weed killer may have to be applied repeatedly to exhaust the supply of starch stored in the root.
CONTROL: Patrol for and pull or kill these weeds at least once a year before they come into flower. If you can't remove them, at least keep the flowers cut off so new seed isn't formed. After pulling the weeds, maintain a thick mulch or apply a preemergence herbicide to prevent germination of the many seeds deposited in the area. Some clump-forming weeds have shallow, fibrous root systems and are relatively easy to pull. Others are harder to pull, such as dandelion, some tree seedlings with taproots, and plants that grow from bulbs, such as wild garlic. Overcoming taprooted and bulbous members of this group also requires follow-up because they can regenerate from bits of root or bulb left behind.
OTHER WEEDS IN THIS GROUP: Flea-bane, pokeweed, violets.

SHALLOW-ROOTED RUNNING PERENNIALS

REPRESENTATIVE: Ground ivy. This plant snakes through lawns, rooting where its stems contact bare soil. In gardens, freed from a mower's restraint, it explodes to become a dense mat, weaving its way 18 inches up into stems of other plants. Its shallow roots are easily pried loose, but it must also be banned from adjacent lawns or it will reinvade. The broad-leaf weed killer Trimec kills it; be sure to overseed and thicken the lawn with better care, or ground ivy seed will return.

CONTROL: Many weeds in this group are like ground ivy—they are easily pulled, apparently with all roots intact. Look closely, though, to see whether pieces of the running roots have broken loose to sprout again. Loosen the soil throughout the area before pulling; apply mulch or preemergence herbicide to prevent recolonization by seed; revisit the area within two weeks to remove sprouted root pieces. Weed barriers are not effective against most of these weeds, which can creep over barriers in just a fraction of an inch of mulch or leaves.

OTHER WEEDS IN THIS GROUP: Catnip, dead nettle, enchanter's nightshade, poison ivy, sour sorrel, violets.

DEEP-ROOTED RUNNING PERENNIALS

REPRESENTATIVE: Canada thistle. Roots run deep and are very brittle. Like some of the other worst weeds in this category, they can persist and resprout for as long as two years, despite frequent pulling or spraying with herbicide

CONTROL: You must be more persistent than these plants to beat their extensive root systems. Pulling, cutting, and herbicide applications put a drain on the roots' starch reserves, but with each day in the sun, new shoots replenish those roots. So loosen the soil well and remove all the foliage and as much root as possible. Then return every four to seven days through at least a full season to pull, cut, or apply a systemic herbicide such as glyphosate to the new sprouts. Don't attack just a few times and then turn away for the rest of the season; survivors will surface, grow, and regain all lost ground. Fall is a time plants move food reserves into their roots. A final glyphosate spray in fall is especially effective.

OTHER WEEDS IN THIS GROUP: Bindweed, field horsetail, milkweed, fleeceflower, quackgrass.

Dandelion's deep root draws nutrients that have leached below many plants' reach, so view pulled dandelions as salvaged nutrients—dry them out and compost them.

If you remove ground ivy from a bed but allow it to remain in an adjacent lawn, it will reinvade.

When poison ivy first begins to creep into a bed, it is easy to pull. Cover your skin before touching it. Wash thoroughly afterward.

Canada thistle roots break easily when pulled. They store a lot of starch and can resprout from even the tiniest pieces.

Although it's not native, quackgrass is so fast-spreading and adaptable that it has become a weed almost everywhere in eastern North America.

Bindweed has an extensive root system. Sprouts may surface from root remnants after two years of hard weeding.

Field horsetail or scouring rush fools gardeners. Loosen an area well so that you remove the horizontal running roots as well as the easily pulled vertical pieces.

PLANT GALLERY

This section features more than a hundred of the finest perennials you can grow. Check here to learn about each plant's preferred growing conditions, how to place it for best effect, special needs, and tips for day-to-day care. Plants are listed in alphabetical order by scientific name.

SCIENTIFIC NAME: A plant's universally accepted name. Use this term when you want to avoid any cases of mistaken identity, such as when searching nursery catalogs, garden centers, or reference books.

COMMON NAME: An everyday name for a particular plant. Be aware that one plant may have many common names, and one common name may apply to several plants. To avoid the confusion when discussing perennials with gardeners in other areas, you may have to exchange not just the common name but the scientific name or detailed descriptions of the leaf and flower to be certain you are discussing the same plant.

LIGHT REQUIRED: How much sun a plant requires each day to maintain good health, develop to expectation, and bloom well. Measure the amount of sun only during the actual growing season.
- **Full sun:** Six or more hours of direct sun.
- **Half sun:** Four to six hours of direct sun.
- **Shade:** Two to four hours of direct sun.
- **Dense shade:** Up to two hours of sun.

SOIL AND DRAINAGE: It's noted here whether a plant grows best in a certain type of soil or responds better where water drains more slowly or more quickly through soil.

MOISTURE: Some perennials grow best if the soil around their roots is allowed to dry down between waterings. Others are healthiest if the soil is constantly moist. Specific water needs are listed for each plant.
- **Continuously moist:** Water whenever necessary to keep the soil around a plant from drying out. (It should never be soggy.)
- **Average water:** Water as soon as the soil in the root zone is dry and warm 2 to 3 inches below the surface.
- **Allow to dry down:** Water after the soil around a plant has been dry and warm 2 to 3 inches below the surface for one or more days.

- **Tolerates drought:** Once established, a plant can survive long periods without rain or supplemental water.
- **Tolerates soggy soil:** A plant can grow even if the soil is waterlogged at times.

DEADHEAD, DIVIDE, AND STAKE: "Day-to-Day Care" explains the terms for these categories. See page 34, staking, page 36, deadheading, and page 40, dividing.

HARDINESS: Hardiness is a measure of cold tolerance; it does not mean how well a plant fends off diseases or pests. Every plant species has a temperature threshold below which it cannot survive. The range of numbers given for each plant corresponds to regions shown on the hardiness zone map of the United States Department of Agriculture (USDA), found at the back of the book.

FAMILY: Closely related plant species are grouped in families. Plants in the same family may have similar-looking flowers, but it's more important to know that plants within a group tend to be susceptible to the same diseases and insect problems. If diseases or insects prey on a perennial, it's wise to replace it with a plant from a different family.

BLOOMS: This tells you the season to expect the plant to be in peak bloom, and the color or range of colors of the flowers. Bloom time may vary with the weather by as much as a week or two from year to year.

Spring may begin six weeks earlier and be more prolonged in southern areas, and commence later and pass more quickly in northern regions. Fall begins about the same time all over the continent, but ends earlier in northern areas than in southern ones. Thus, seasons are defined by the plants in bloom during the season as well as by date. (Note: Dates given are for Zones 5 and 6.)
- **Early spring:** From the bloom of snowdrops and witch hazels until forsythia blooms (roughly March 1–April 15).
- **Midspring:** From forsythia's peak bloom until flowering dogwood begins to show significant color (roughly April 15–May 15).
- **Late spring:** From peak flowering dogwood season until peony is in full bloom (roughly May 15–June 15).

The garden is gorgeous at the height of summer. Entries in this plant gallery explain what the plants in your garden need to be beautiful all year.

■ **Early summer:** From the first big display of large-flowered clematis and Hybrid Tea roses until Shasta daisies come into peak bloom (roughly June 15–July 15).

■ **Midsummer:** From the time Shasta daisies peak and blue or pink hydrangeas are in full bloom until rose of Sharon comes into peak bloom (roughly July 15–August 8).

■ **Late summer:** From the first show of field goldenrod until roadside purple asters bloom (roughly August 8–September 1).

■ **Fall:** From the full bloom of 'Autumn Joy' sedum until burning bushes turn red and silver maple leaves turn color (roughly September 1–late October).

SHAPE, SIZE, AND GROWTH RATE: Shape is the form of a plant in the garden (carpet-forming, mounded, vase, or columnar). Size refers to height and width. Information includes whether a plant stays in one place (forms a clump), travels (spreading), or travels a lot (invasive). Growth rate means how long a perennial takes to reach full size.

■ **Slow:** Width or number of stems may increase only 10 to 25 percent in a year.

■ **Moderate:** Increases by 25 to 50 percent in spread or number of stems in a year.

■ **Fast:** Doubles in spread or number of stems in a season or less.

■ **Very fast:** More than doubles in spread or number of stems in a season or less.

ENVIRONMENTAL NOTES: Additional information about soil, drainage, and site.

USES: How a perennial complements other plants in the garden. Suggested combinations are based more on season-long qualities—shape, foliage color, and texture—than on bloom, which may last only a few weeks.

CARE: Explains specialized maintenance that deviates from standard care noted in "Day-to-Day Care" (such as information about insects and diseases, fertilizer, staking methods, or deadheading, pinching, or cutting back).

NOTES: Includes practical information, such as whether the plant is poisonous. Outstanding varieties and related species are also noted.

ACANTHUS SPINOSUS

Spiny bear's breeches

3-4'

4'

- Full to half sun; midday shade in hot regions
- Well-drained, slightly acid to neutral soil

Spiny bear's breeches

- Dry down; tolerates drought, heat, and humidity
- Deadhead as standard spike
- Divide spring or fall; not usually needed; running
- Staking unnecessary
- Zones 5–10, Zone 6 if drainage is poor
- Acanthus family

BLOOMS: Blooms for four to six weeks, late spring (South) or early summer (North). White flowers with dusky maroon jackets.

SHAPE, SIZE, GROWTH RATE: Impressive clump-forming mound with large, dark green leaves and spires of flowers. Grows slowly at first, then picks up speed to a moderate pace. Has potential to form a large colony. Evergreen in warm regions.

ENVIRONMENTAL NOTES: In warmer areas, provide some shade during the heat of the day; may bloom less than in cooler regions.

USES: Combines well with cushion spurge and pearly everlasting. Blooms at same time as daylily,

meadowsweet, and balloon flower.

CARE: Spiny bear's breeches are generally pest-free, but slugs and snails may be a problem. New plants can be obtained by digging near the crown in spring, cutting off pencil-thin roots several inches long, and planting them vertically just below soil level, with the cut end up. Unintentional root cuttings—broken bits of root—can surge up and reclaim a bed, should you ever decide to dig it out. Deadheading is optional; no repeat bloom will be produced, and flowering stalks can be attractive after bloom. Cut plants back in late fall (cold areas) or early spring (warmer ones).

NOTES: A living sculpture of sturdy 4-foot spikes of white flowers and huge, dark, glossy leaves that were models for the carving at the tops of classical Corinthian columns. Leaves are spined and thistlelike but not really dangerous. Avoid hiding this big plant at the back of the border; set it in the middle or even the front if your design can accommodate it.

ACHILLEA

Yarrow

1½-4'

1½'

- Full sun
- Well-drained soil; soil type and pH adaptable; avoid poor drainage
- Average moisture; tolerates drought, heat, and salt
- Deadhead as branched flower
- Divide in spring or fall; clump-formers: offsets, four to five

years; those with running roots: two years; easy to move
- Grow-through supports
- Zones 3–9
- Aster family

BLOOMS: From late spring into midsummer. Ferny foliage and distinctive flat-topped flower clusters in yellow, white, red, pink, or pastel.

SHAPE, SIZE, GROWTH RATE: Varies. Some are mounded in leaf, columnar in bloom; others form

mats. 18- to 24-inch varieties are as tall as wide; varieties taller than that are half as tall as wide. Fast.

USES: Combines well with false indigo, bell flower, crocosmia, iris delphinium, coneflower, daylily.

CARE: Basically pest-free. Powdery mildew and stem and root rots may occur in wet or very dry soil. Rabbit- and deer-resistant. Apply fertilizer at half the average rate. Cut stems to the ground after bloom season ends to encourage new basal foliage. Cut back in early spring or late fall.

At 36 inches, 'Coronation Gold' fern leaf yarrow (A. filipendula) is unlikely to need staking.

'Moonshine' (A. × taygeta) blooms earlier than others but is short-lived in heat and humidity. It grows 24 inches tall.

Common yarrow (A. millefolium) blooms early, spreads aggressively, and needs staking if nights are above 70° F.

ACONITUM CARMICHAELII

Monkshood

3-4' / 2'

- Full sun to shade; midday shade in hot areas
- Well-drained, organic-matter-enriched clay soil
- Constantly moist; does not do well in heat, nighttime temperatures above 70° F
- Deadhead as a top-down spike
- Divide immediately after bloom in fall; rarely needed; eyes; hard to move; slow to reestablish
- Grow-through stake or none
- Zones 3–8; mulch deeply in

- Zones 3 and 4
- Buttercup family

BLOOMS: Blue flowers in late summer or fall.
SHAPE, SIZE, GROWTH RATE: Four feet is typical but may reach 6 feet. Clump-forming. Slow-growing at first; moderate once established.
USES: Pair with goatsbeard and fragrant bugbane. Blooms at same time as Japanese anemone.
CARE: Apply 50 percent more fertilizer than for average plants. Wilting in early spring indicates crown rot; improve winter drainage. Check for bacterial leaf spot and mildew in midspring; remove infected leaves and apply fungicide.

Cyclamen mite may be a problem. Deadheading prolongs bloom in areas with long fall. Resistant to rabbits and deer. Cut back to the ground in late fall. Remove and destroy prunings to prevent disease.
NOTES: Plant is poisonous.

'Bressingham Spire', 3 feet tall and violet-blue, blooms earlier and is more floriferous than the species.

ACTAEA RUBRA

Red baneberry

2-3' / 2'

- Half sun to dense shade
- Well-drained, organic soil
- Constant to average moisture; tolerates drought but not heat
- No deadheading; seed heads are attractive
- Divide in spring; forked taproot; division rarely needed
- Staking unnecessary

- Zones 4–8
- Buttercup family

BLOOMS: Bottlebrush white flowers in late spring.
SHAPE, SIZE, GROWTH RATE: Coarse mound of light green foliage. Clump-forming. Flowers and berries held above foliage. Slow growing.
USES: Combines well with the shapes and textures of heart-leaf brunnera, Jacob's ladder, and lungwort. Blooms with coral bells, Solomon's seal, and globeflower.
CARE: No special fertilizer needs. Basically pest-free. Cut back to the ground in late fall. For more plants, sow fresh seed in early fall after

soaking berries to remove pulp from seed. Requires several weeks of 70° F temperatures, then several months at or below 40° F, and a gradual warm-up in spring for complete germination.
NOTES: Berries are toxic.

Red baneberry

AGASTACHE FOENICULUM

Anise hyssop

2½-4' / 1½'

- Full sun to shade
- Well-drained, slightly alkaline soil
- Average water; tolerates drought, heat
- Deadhead as standard spike
- Divide in spring every three to four years, offsets
- Staking unnecessary except when grown in shade; individual braces for most natural look
- Zones 5–9; less hardy with

poor drainage; some hybrids hardy only to Zone 7
- Mint family

BLOOMS: Mid- to late summer. Dense, finger-long spikes of lavender-blue.
SHAPE, SIZE, GROWTH RATE: Columnar 30 to 48 inches tall. Spreading. Increases in size at moderate to fast pace.
USES: Complements shapes and textures of peony, black-eyed Susan, phlox, and meadow rue. Blooms with late-season daylilies, bee balm, and purple coneflower.
CARE: Requires no special fertilizer treatments. Has few pest or disease problems. May suffer from powdery

mildew in hot, dry years; increase water to counter. Rabbit- and deer-resistant. Cut back plants to the ground in late fall. Reseeds readily.
NOTES: 'Blue Fortune' grows 4 feet or taller. 'Firebird' has interesting salmon to pink flowers; may be hardy only to Zone 6.

Anise hyssop

ALCHEMILLA MOLLIS

Lady's mantle

12"

18"

- Half sun to shade
- Well-drained, moisture-retentive soil
- Constantly moist to average moisture
- Cut back flower stalks as seed begins to turn brown
- Divide spring, offsets; easy to move; can be grown from seed
- Staking unnecessary
- Zones 4–8
- Rose family

BLOOMS: From late spring to early summer, this plant produces a froth of tiny yellow-green flowers.

SHAPE, SIZE, GROWTH RATE: Dense mound of coarse, downy, light green foliage. Foliage is a main attraction, each leaf emerging like pleated velvet and fanning into a circle. Flower stalks rise 8 to 12 inches above the leaves. Clump-forming. Moderate growth rate.

USES: Shape and foliage combine well with fringed bleeding heart or toad lily. Blooms with bellflowers, Oriental poppies, and large-flowered clematis.

CARE: No special fertilizer needs. Basically pest-free, but plant bug may disfigure foliage. Old foliage can be stripped off in early spring, but do not cut back hard because new growth buds form on the semiwoody crown above ground. Where summers are very hot and humid, lady's mantle is prone to leaf diseases. Can be cleaned up in spring by mowing to 4 inches high; tolerates light foot traffic.

NOTES: Easy-care perennial. Soft green complements any color.

Dwarf lady's mantle (*A. alpina*) is only 12 inches tall in bloom. The underside of each deeply lobed leaf has fine hairs that extend beyond the edge to create a silky, silvery outline.

Lady's mantle

ANAPHALIS TRIPLINERVIS

Pearly everlasting

18"

24"

- Full to half sun
- Best in well-drained, sandy soil but tolerant of a range of soil conditions
- Average water; tolerates excess moisture far better than most gray-foliage plants
- Deadhead as branched flower
- Grow-through stakes
- Divide every four to five years, running; easy to move
- Zones 4–8
- Aster family

BLOOMS: Midsummer into late summer. Clusters of white pearls open to yellow-centered buttons with crisp papery petals.

SHAPE, SIZE, GROWTH RATE: Mounded shape, 12 to 18 inches tall; may grow taller if moisture is plentiful. Medium texture; spreading; fast growth.

ENVIRONMENTAL NOTES: Does not grow well where summers are very hot and humid.

USES: Its mounded shape and gray foliage combine well with bear's breeches, speedwell, threadleaf coreopsis, and 'Husker Red' penstemon. Attracts butterflies.

CARE: Basically pest-free but may host larvae of the American Painted Lady butterfly during spring and early summer. Protect new plantings from these leaf-eating caterpillars, but tolerate them on established plants if you can; the caterpillars finish feeding in time for the plant to recover and bloom well. Dried flowers are attractive on plant. Rust sometimes develops; deer- and rabbit-resistant. Apply fertilizer at half the average rate to avoid rank, weak growth. Cut back to the ground in late fall.

NOTES: The dwarf cultivar 'Summer Snow' is a good edging plant, often less than 12 inches tall.

A related North American species, *A. margaritacea*, is native to dry meadows and slopes. It is more drought-tolerant and should be considered for such situations, but it is less able than the other species to tolerate heavy or wet soils. *A. margaritacea* is taller (up to 36 inches), later-blooming by two weeks, and less likely to need staking; it has narrower leaves than *A. triplinervis*. Japanese pearly everlasting (*A. margaritacea* var. *yedoensis*) has larger flowers than the species and may be hardy to Zone 3 with good snow cover.

Pearly everlasting

ANEMONE X HYBRIDA

Japanese anemone

3-5'
2'

- Sun to shade
- Well-drained soil; excels in well-drained moisture-retentive loam
- Average to constant moisture. Does not tolerate wet soil or drought
- Deadhead to prolong bloom; branched flower
- Divide in spring or fall every four to five years, running
- Some varieties may need staking, with individual braces
- Zones 5–8
- Buttercup family

BLOOMS: Blooms late summer into fall; earlier in sunny sites than in shade. Flower buds, like soft pink or white pearls, are attractive before bloom. White, pink, or mauve petals form a wide cup around a button center fringed with golden stamens. Flowers are held high above foliage.

SHAPE, SIZE, GROWTH RATE: Mounded 2-foot basal foliage sends up branching flower stalks in June. Flowers may rise 3 feet higher. Plant increases size slowly the first season. Once established, some varieties grow at a moderate rate, others very fast and may become invasive.

ENVIRONMENTAL NOTES: Hardy in Zone 4 with heavy mulch or reliable snow cover. Performs poorly where summers are hot or winds strong.

USES: Attractive with turtlehead and Japanese wax bell in shade; purple bush clover and culver's root in half sun. Do not plant with small, clump-forming perennials, which get lost in anemone's spread.

CARE: Reduced vigor from nematode infestation and pock-marked foliage from four-lined plant bug feeding can be problems. Rabbit-resistant. May topple in light, dry soil. Some varieties have stouter stems that rarely require support. Spreads by underground rhizomes and can form large, dense colonies.

Rarely sets viable seed. Cut back in late fall.

NOTES: 'Honorine Jobert', pure white, 3 to 4 feet tall. Flowers are smaller than those on other varieties. 'Queen Charlotte', semidouble pale mauve flowers, 3 feet. 'Whirlwind', semidouble large white flowers, 3 to 5 feet. 'Margarette', semidouble, deep pink, 2 to 3 feet.

Grapeleaf anemone (*A. tomentosa*) is white or pale pink and 18 to 36 inches.

Japanese anemone

ANTHEMIS TINCTORIA

Golden marguerite

2-3'
3'

- Full to half sun
- Well-drained soil; tolerates alkaline soil
- Average water; tolerates drought and heat
- Deadhead to prolong bloom and prevent seed set, branched flower
- Divide every two to three years before oldest, central portion of clump dies out; offsets; easy to move
- Stake with crutches or grow-through supports
- Zones 3–8
- Aster family

BLOOMS: Bright yellow daisies in cheery masses from early to midsummer.

SHAPE, SIZE, GROWTH RATE: Very fast-growing; spreads by ground-level offsets and seed.

USES: Finely divided deep green foliage and upright habit combine well with heart-leaf brunnera, artemisia, daylily, tall sedum, and fountain grass. Border specimen, cut flower, fragrant foliage.

CARE: Basically pest-free but may develop powdery mildew and can itself become a pest by self-sowing. Cut back after bloom fades to promote new basal growth. Apply fertilizer at half the average rate to avoid soft, floppy growth. Easy to grow from seed or division. Cut back to the ground in late fall.

NOTES: 'Moonlight' is 2 feet tall and has pale yellow flowers. Foliage is more finely cut on 'Kelwayi'; it is taller (3 feet), with brighter yellow flowers. 'E. C. Buxton' has pale off-white to lemon-yellow flowers and finely cut foliage; it is 2 to 3 feet tall.

Marguerite daisy

AQUILEGIA X HYBRIDA

Columbine

1-3'

1'

- Half to full sun; midday shade prolongs bloom
- Well-drained, sandy loam; prefers neutral to slightly acid pH
- Average moisture
- Deadhead to prolong bloom
- Divide in early spring every three years, forked taproot

'McKana hybrids' are dependable performers with pastel flowers. They grow 18 to 30 inches tall.

- Staking unnecessary
- Zones 4–9
- Buttercup family

BLOOMS: Blooms midspring. Many colors and color combinations from yellow, salmon, red, blue, and white. Blue-flowered varieties tend to bloom later than others.

SHAPE, SIZE, GROWTH RATE: Mounded foliage topped by sturdy, upright, branched flower stalks, which double or triple the height of the plant. Plants may be 1 to 3 feet tall in bloom. Clump-forming; fast.

ENVIRONMENTAL NOTES: Tolerates alkaline soil. Red-flowered types with hanging blooms generally require wetter soil and are intolerant of drought. Blue-flowered types descend from the western or Rocky Mountain columbine (*A. caerulea*) so prefer more sun and cooler summers. They also tolerate drier soil.

USES: Flowers combine with foam flower and woodland phlox. Medium-textured foliage is a good foil for toad lily and tovara.

CARE: Columbine grows readily from seed, which requires a period of dry, warm storage (such as on the plant) before it will germinate. Fertilize more heavily than the average perennial. Cut back in late fall. Columbine is relatively short-lived. Check leaves as flower buds swell for leaf-miner damage, which appears as light-colored squiggles in the leaf; keep in check by cutting plants back hard right after bloom and destroying the cuttings. Species columbine, particularly the bicolored red and yellow Canadian columbine (*A. canadensis*), may be resistant to leaf miner. Columbine sawfly can defoliate plants in early summer. Look for wormlike pale green larvae on leaves at bloom time. Occasional problems include powdery mildew, leaf spots, aphids, columbine stalk borer, and crown rot, where soil is wet in winter or drainage is poor. Don't let all these problems discourage you from growing columbine; it is a beautiful plant.

ARABIS CAUCASICA

Wall rockcress

8"

18"

- Half to full sun
- Must have well-drained loam and neutral or slightly alkaline pH to thrive
- Average moisture
- Deadhead by shearing to promote density
- Divide every two to three years in early fall, running or loose offsets; easy to move
- Zones 4–8
- Mustard family

BLOOMS: White flowers in early spring.

SHAPE, SIZE, GROWTH RATE: Mat-forming grayish evergreen spreads by rooting where its stems contact moist soil. Forms colonies at moderate to fast rate—a well-sited 6-inch-wide plant may be 18 inches wide at the end of a season.

ENVIRONMENTAL NOTES: Does not grow well where summers are very hot and humid; tends to develop crown and stem rot.

USES: Attractive with columbine, masterwort, and lungwort. Pair with other evergreen perennials such as coral bells.

CARE: Apply fertilizer at half the average rate. Powdery mildew, rust, and aphids are sometimes a problem. Susceptible to club root. Look for deformed, shortened roots on plants that do not thrive or that decline. Destroy infected plants. Do not plant other members of the mustard family where club root has been a problem. Do not cut back in fall: it's evergreen. Trim as desired in early spring or after bloom.

NOTES: 'Flore Pleno' has double flowers, is later to bloom than the species, and tends to stay in bloom longer.

Rock cress

ARMERIA MARITIMA

Sea thrift

6"
6"

- Full sun; in areas with very hot, humid summers, afternoon shade is recommended
- Must have well-drained soil; prefers sandy soil with neutral to slightly alkaline pH
- Average moisture
- Reblooms in cool climates if deadheaded; head
- Divide in fall; infrequent; taproot; propagate by division; roots readily from cuttings and grows easily from seed
- Staking unnecessary
- Zones 3–8
- Plumbago family

BLOOMS: Midspring. Spherical clusters of flowers in shades of pink or creamy white, rising above foliage.

SHAPE, SIZE, GROWTH RATE: The grassy tuft of evergreen foliage is 6 inches tall and may spread to nearly 2 feet in width, much like a clean, deep green cushion. Flower stalks double the height. Clump-forming. Moderate growth rate.

ENVIRONMENTAL NOTES: Good for windy sites. Salt-tolerant. Cannot tolerate wet soil in winter.

USES: This deep green mound goes well with the gray-green foliage of Cupid's dart and swordlike spears of iris or blackberry lily. Blooms with catmint.

CARE: Apply fertilizer at half the average rate. Heavy fertilization causes the center of the clump to blacken and die. Basically pest-free. Do not cut back in fall: it's evergreen.

NOTES: 'Ruby Glow' flowers are nearly red. 'Dusseldorf Pride' flowers are deep rose but this variety may not be as cold-hardy as the species; protect it with an airy, deep mulch in areas colder than Zone 5.

Pinkball thrift (*A. pseudarmeria*) is taller by several inches and has larger flower heads ideal for cut flowers and drying. This species is hardy in Zones 6–8. Pyrenees thrift (*A. caespitosa* 'Bevan's Variety') is a 4-inch-tall dwarf. Its pink flowers are nearly stemless.

Sea thrift

ARTEMISIA LUDOVICIANA

White sage

3-4'
4'+

- Full sun
- Any well-drained soil; neutral to slightly alkaline pH
- Average moisture; tolerates drought
- Deadheading not necessary
- Divide every three years, discarding the oldest, central portion; running
- Grow-through stake sometimes necessary
- Zones 4–9
- Aster family

BLOOMS: Grown for magnificent gray-green foliage, not flowers. In late summer, inconspicuous small whitish flowers develop.

SHAPE, SIZE, GROWTH RATE: Although wider than tall, the plant gives overall impression of vertical lines. Spreads by shallow rhizomes. Very fast growth rate.

ENVIRONMENTAL NOTES: Doesn't flourish where summers are very humid.

USES: Backdrop for blue and purple flowers, such as speedwell, blue columbine, and perennial salvia and purple-foliage plants. Tones down harsh red and orange flowers.

CARE: Apply fertilizer at half the average rate. May need staking in rich soils. Stem and root rots can be a problem if the summer is hot and humid or drainage poor. Painted Lady butterfly caterpillars may feed on artemisia. Leaf rust sometimes occurs. Deer- and rabbit-resistant. Reduce spread as desired in spring. Stem cuttings taken in midsummer root readily. Seed requires dry, warm storage for several months before it will germinate. Cut back in late fall.

NOTES: Often confused with dusty miller, crushed white sage leaves have a distinct scent.

White mugwort (A. lactiflora) is the only green-leaved artemisia. 'Guizho' grows 4 to 6 feet tall, Zones 3–9.

White sage grows aggressively but 'Valerie Finnis', shown here, is a clump-former.

Hardy in Zones 4–8, 'Silver Mound' artemisia (A. schmidtiana) does best in cool summers; 12–15 inches tall.

ARUNCUS DIOICUS

Goatsbeard

4-6'

3-4'

- Half sun to dense shade; tolerates full sun if shaded during the hottest part of day
- Any well-drained soil
- Average moisture; faster growth with extra water; drought-tolerant
- Do not deadhead until you see if you like the seed heads, which can be attractive
- Rarely needs division; offsets
- Staking unnecessary
- Zones 4–8
- Rose family

Goatsbeard

BLOOMS: Airy off-white plumes from late spring to early summer.

SHAPE, SIZE, GROWTH RATE: Can be mistaken for a small shrub. Slow to moderate growth rate.

USES: Combine this upright, medium-textured plant with mounded perennials such as geranium or bleeding hearts. Play its light green foliage off of darker green turtlehead or blue-green hostas. Use its sturdy stems to support a blue-bush clematis or other clematis that can be cut back hard every spring.

CARE: Basically pest-free. Leaf spot, rust, or leaf scorch may develop, usually where the site is too dry or hot. Resistant to deer and rabbit damage. Dense, almost woody root system requires saw to divide. Transplant does not require pampering. Male and female flowers occur on separate plants. Goatsbeard may self-sow but not to a troublesome degree. Cut back in late fall, or wait until early spring if the stems and seed heads are desired for winter interest.

NOTES: The cultivar 'Kneiffii' is just 3 feet tall in bloom. Half the height is flower stalk. Foliage is finely cut and lacy.

Dwarf goatsbeard (*A. aethusifolius*) is a delightful miniature just 12 inches tall in bloom—a mound of finely cut foliage and dainty white spike flowers. Blooms two weeks earlier than the species. Dwarf goatsbeard is a good edging plant.

ASCLEPIAS TUBEROSA

Butterfly weed

1½-2

1½-2'

- Full sun
- Requires excellent drainage; prefers sandy soil
- Average moisture, but allow to dry down between waterings; tolerates drought
- Reblooms several weeks later if deadheaded; tip cluster
- Staking unnecessary
- Rarely needs division; forked taproot
- Zones 4–9
- Milkweed family

BLOOMS: Bright orange flowers in flaring clusters in midsummer. Individual flowers are just ¼ inch across but worth close inspection. A butterfly's leg slips in easily and the flower hangs onto it. As the butterfly struggles to pull free, it is dusted with pollen, ensuring pollination of the next plant in its path.

SHAPE, SIZE, GROWTH RATE: Sturdy, vase-shaped plant, 18 to 24 inches tall and equally wide. Clump-forming and long-lived. Slow to grow.

ENVIRONMENTAL NOTES: Must have considerable heat to prosper and bloom well, so not suited for cool summer climates. Intolerant of wet soil in winter.

USES: Combine this moderately coarse-textured, vase-shaped perennial with finer-textured mounded plants, such as catmint, sheep's fescue, blue oat grass, fountain grass, or threadleaf coreopsis. For contrast, plant it with coarser gray-leaved ornamental mullein or globe thistle.

CARE: Apply fertilizer at half the average rate. The taproot is daunting to some but is simple to divide by cutting through the top to obtain several bud eyes and a large slice of the root. Cuttings can also be made from pencil-thick roots. Plants are basically pest-free. They may suffer from aphid infestation; check drainage if this is the case. Butterfly weed is slow to emerge in spring. Mark its spot so you don't plant on top of it. Cut back in late fall.

NOTES: Monarch butterflies feed on this plant, so it's prudent to tolerate some leaf damage if you are encouraging butterflies.

Mauve-flowering swamp milkweed (*A. incarnata*) is also a Monarch host plant but is a native of wet areas. Grow it for midsummer bloom and to attract butterflies in heavy, wet clay soil.

Butterfly weed

ASTER NOVAE-ANGLIAE

New England aster

1½–6'
3'

- Full to half sun
- Most garden soils
- Constant to average moisture for best growth; tolerates drought
- Deadhead to prolong bloom; branched flower
- Divide every two to three years in spring to control spread and renew plant vigor; discard oldest, central section; offset
- Tall varieties may need staking; stake individual stems or provide horizontal grow-through support
- Zones 4–8
- Aster family

BLOOMS: Late summer and fall; start of bloom depends on variety. Gardeners in coldest regions should not select latest-blooming varieties because plants may be cut down by a freeze. White and a wide range of violets, pinks, and near-blues.

SHAPE, SIZE, GROWTH RATE: Mounded dwarf (18 to 24 inches tall and wide); or tall columnar plants (up to 6 feet tall and half as wide). Fast to very fast growth rate. Spreads by shallow rhizomes.

USES: Plant with ornamental grasses, sedum, or and Joe-Pye weed. Plant over crocus and other minor, early bulbs. Combine dwarf asters with blazing star or daylilies.

CARE: Easy to grow from seed. Some varieties self-sow. Divide every two to three years in spring to control spread and renew plant vigor; discard oldest, central section. Replant small five- to seven-eye divisions for strongest stems and best disease resistance.

Pinch plants monthly from midspring to early summer for shorter, denser plants. More likely to need staking in half sun if light is strongly one-directional. Take measures to protect from rabbits, deer, and woodchucks. Powdery mildew and rust can be problems; check watering to avoid dry soil and wet foliage. Wilt can infect older plantings; grow new plants from tip cuttings in a bed that has not recently hosted an aster family member. Plants attract Japanese beetles, occasionally stalk borers. Cut back in late fall. If seeds are intended as winter forage for birds, wait until early spring to cut back.

NOTES: 'Alma Potschke' blooms are red-violet, 3 to 4 feet. Dark purple 'Purple Dome' grows to 18 inches.

Dwarf 'Wood's Pink' aster

ASTILBE X ARENDSII

Astilbe

1–3'
1–3'

- Half sun to shade; tolerates sun if soil is constantly moist
- Rich loam with organic matter; neutral to acid pH
- Constantly moist to wet soil
- Don't deadhead if seed heads desired for winter interest. Early-blooming varieties will rebloom if deadheaded; spike
- Rarely needs division; offsets
- Staking unnecessary
- Zones 4–8
- Rockfoil family

BLOOMS: Early to midsummer. White, pink, red, and mauve. Flower cluster may be a tight, upright spike; a compact steeple; or a loose, drooping plume.

SHAPE, SIZE, GROWTH RATE: Mound of ferny bronze to green foliage. Flower stalks double height—15 to 36 inches tall and wide. Clump-forming. Slow to moderate growth.

USES: Texture contrasts with coarse-textured plants and form with upright plants. Hosta, lungwort, rodgersia, Japanese wax bell, toad lily, turtlehead, and meadow rue are good companions.

CARE: Tolerates many soil types and wide pH range if the moisture needs are met. Apply 50 percent more fertilizer than for average perennials. Vulnerable to powdery mildew, leaf scorch, rust, Japanese beetles, spider mites, and root weevils. Divide in spring or fall; use sharp tool to cut woody crown into sections with several eyes each; watch for wilting after moving; hard to move. Long-lived. Cut back in early spring or late fall.

'Deutschland', an early summer bloomer, grows to 24 inches.

A mid-season bloomer, 'Erica' grows 3 feet tall.

'Glut' blooms in midsummer and grows to 18 inches.

Late-blooming Chinese astilbe (A. chinensis) takes drier soil. Zones 4–8.

ASTRANTIA MAJOR

Great masterwort

18-36"
18"
■ Half to full sun; increase water in full sun

'Hadspen Blood' masterwort

■ Rich, well-drained loam with plenty of organic matter
■ Average to constant moisture
■ Deadhead for prolonged and repeat bloom; branched flower
■ Rarely needs division
■ Staking unnecessary
■ Zones 4–9
■ Carrot family

BLOOMS: Late spring to early summer. White, pink, and rose flowers form domed clusters above petal-like bracts.
SHAPE, SIZE, GROWTH RATE: Mounded foliage 15 to 18 inches tall. Flowers rise 12 to 18 inches higher on wiry, branched stems. Dense clump that also spreads by underground rhizomes. Slow to moderate growth rate.
ENVIRONMENTAL NOTES: Does not tolerate drought or regions where summer nights are hot.
USES: Foil for Siberian iris, feather reed grass, white gaura, and perennial flax. Combines well with peony and perennial salvia.
CARE: Apply 50 percent more fertilizer than for average perennials. Basically pest-free. Protect from rabbits and woodchucks. Cut back foliage in late fall or early spring to avoid leaf spot. If not deadheaded, will self-sow but not to nuisance levels.

BAPTISIA AUSTRALIS

Blue false indigo

False indigo

4'
4'
■ Full to half sun
■ Deep, well-drained soil with plentiful organic matter
■ Average moisture
■ Will not rebloom after deadheading
■ Rarely needs division, deep offsets; difficult to move
■ In shade, use grow-through supports
■ Zones 3–9
■ Pea family

BLOOMS: Blue-violet flowers on tall spikes in midspring. Blue-black pea pods persist through winter.
SHAPE, SIZE, GROWTH RATE: Clump-forming; 3 to 4 feet tall and equally wide; tends to have bare ankles. Slow grower.
ENVIRONMENTAL NOTES: Drought- and heat-tolerant. Poor growth in alkaline soil.
USES: Good companion to sword-leaf inula, perennial geranium, hardy ageratum, and black-eyed Susan. Winter stems complement ornamental grasses and gray-foliaged perennials such as Russian sage.
CARE: Generally pest-free. Rabbits may browse flower stalks. Voles may eat roots during winter. Cut back in late fall or early spring if left for winter interest.
NOTES: 'Purple Smoke' has charcoal-green stems contrasting with pale lilac flowers, 3 to 4 feet tall; Zones 3–8.

BELAMCANDA CHINENSIS

Blackberry lily

Blackberry lily

18-40"
18"
■ Full to half sun
■ Well-drained, sandy soil
■ Average moisture
■ Deadhead as tip cluster; seedpods attractive
■ Renew by division in spring every two to three years; running
■ Stake individual stems
■ Zones 5–10
■ Iris family

BLOOMS: Miniature 2-inch-wide orange or yellow-orange with maroon spots in midsummer. Buds open in succession; each bloom lasts a day. In fall, pods open up to show off black seeds.
SHAPE, SIZE, GROWTH RATE: Swordlike foliage, tall flower stalks; 18 to 24 inches in leaf, 30 to 40 inches in bloom. Fast-growing.
ENVIRONMENTAL NOTES: Heat-tolerant. Not a good candidate for areas with cool, moist summers. Does not tolerate wet soil in winter.
USES: Combine with ornamental grasses, cushion spurge, blanket flower, or globe thistle.
CARE: Susceptible to iris borer and iris soft rot. Check for leaf damage in spring; remove and destroy all foliage and stems in fall. Self-sows aggressively. Short-lived.
NOTES: A cousin, candy lily (× *Pardancanda norrisii*), is 30 to 36 inches tall and blooms in violet, cream, orange-red, salmon, or yellow.

BRUNNERA MACROPHYLLA

Heart-leaf brunnera

12-18"   24"

- Shade to dense shade; full sun only in regions with cool summers and steady moisture
- Well-drained soil
- Average to constant moisture
- Deadheading not needed except to prevent self-sowing
- Divide as needed every four to five years as clumps age; running
- Staking unnecessary
- Zones 4–8
- Forget-me-not family

BLOOMS: Tiny sky blue flowers with yellow centers in early to midspring.

SHAPE, SIZE, GROWTH RATE: Low mound of coarse foliage, 12 inches by 24 inches wide; 18 inches tall in bloom. Spreads by rhizomes and seed. Fast growth.

ENVIRONMENTAL NOTES: Drought- and heat-tolerant. Scorches in hot, sunny sites.

USES: Foliage partners well with blue-green, lacy, ferny, and upright plants, such as fringed bleeding heart, fragrant bugbane, and astilbe, perennial flax and Jacob's ladder.

CARE: Basically pest-free. Slug resistant. Dig out excess plants and seedlings annually. Don't leave roots if you're trying to eliminate plants. Deadhead variegated cultivars; seedlings will be green and crowd out the variegated plant.

Heart-leaf brunnera

CAMPANULA CARPATICA

Carpathian bellflower

9-12"   15"

- Full to half sun
- Moist, well-drained soil
- Average to constant moisture
- Deadhead to prolong bloom and promote repeat bloom; branched flower
- Divide in fall or spring every three to five years or when clumps begin to open in center; offset; easy to move
- Staking not needed
- Zones 3–8
- Bellflower family

BLOOMS: Flaring, upturned violet, blue-violet, or white bells. Late spring and early summer.

SHAPE, SIZE, GROWTH RATE: Mounded plants with flowers on wiry, branched stems a few inches above the foliage, 9 to 12 inches tall, 12 to 15 inches wide. Fast growth. Clump-forming.

ENVIRONMENTAL NOTES: Does not tolerate drought, full shade, hot summer nights, or wet soil. Grows in wide pH range.

USES: Beautiful with low-growing plants of varied foliage colors, such as Cupid's dart, 'Moonshine' yarrow, sheep's fescue, thrift, myrtle spurge, 'Vera Jameson' sedum, and pinks. Flowers complement massed tiny flowers, such as heucherella, lavender, and thyme.

CARE: Attracts rabbits and woodchucks. Self-sows. Named varieties often come true from seed. No need to cut back in late fall or early spring, but if slugs and snails are a problem, cut back in late fall.

NOTES: Peach-leaf bellflower (*C. persicifolia*) has white, pink, or violet out-turned bells on wiry, nearly naked stems above fine-textured foliage, 18 to 36 inches in bloom. Vigorous spreader. Less heat-tolerant than shorter bellflowers.

Milky bellflower (C. lactiflora) *has midsummer violet, pink, or white blooms on 3-foot stems (running roots; grow through supports).*

Carpathian bellflower

Clustered bellflower (C. glomerata) *has white or violet flowers in early summer; 12–36 inches tall. Cut back hard after bloom.*

CATANANCHE CAERULEA

Cupid's dart

24"
12"

- Full sun
- Well-drained, sandy soil
- Average moisture, allow to dry down between waterings
- Deadhead to prolong bloom; branched stems
- Divide every two to three years, offsets
- Zones 4–8
- Aster family

BLOOMS: Papery light blue flowers with a dark eye on wiry stems, early summer.

SHAPE, SIZE, GROWTH RATE: Rosette of narrow gray-green foliage hugs the ground. Flower stems rise to 24 inches. Fast growth. Clump-forming.

ENVIRONMENTAL NOTES: Good in windy sites. Heat- and drought-tolerant. Does not tolerate wet soil or high heat and high humidity in summer.

USES: A delicate "see-through" plant with wiry, leafless flower stems above low foliage. Pretty with nonaggressive plants of greater substance as a backdrop or easily controlled spreaders with gray-green foliage, such as sedum, butterfly weed, lamb's-ears, gas plant, 'Silver Brocade' artemisia, and perennial salvia. Interesting interplanted among sheep's fescue.

CARE: Short-lived. Basically pest-free. Does not need to be cut down in late fall or early spring, because stems and foliage decompose rapidly over winter.

NOTES: For white flowers, grow the variety 'Alba'. The scientific name stems from the Greek for powerful incentive. This and the common name refer to the use of the flowers in love potions.

Cupid's dart

CENTAUREA MONTANA

Perennial bachelor's button

12-18"
2'

- Full to half sun
- Any well-drained soil
- Average moisture
- Deadhead to prolong bloom; branched flower
- Divide every two to three years, offsets; or allow some seedlings to grow to renew the planting; easy to move
- Support with short crutches if needed
- Zone 3–8
- Aster family

BLOOMS: Two-inch flowers in midspring; blue-violet with wispy frills radiating from a darker center. Reblooms in midsummer if cut back after first bloom.

SHAPE, SIZE, GROWTH RATE: Mounded, lance-shaped gray-green foliage, 12 to 15 inches tall; topped by flowers on leafy 18-inch stems. Clump-forming; increases by offsets and self-sows readily. Very fast growth.

ENVIRONMENTAL NOTES: Tolerates wind, heat, drought, and high-pH soil but not wet soil, especially in winter.

USES: Mounded, downy foliage fills in around later-emerging, taller and narrower plants, such as balloon flower, Russian sage, checkerbloom, and butterfly weed. Blue flowers combine well with early daisy 'May Queen', candytuft, and Oriental poppy.

CARE: Cut back hard after spring bloom to promote lush new foliage and second bloom in summer and to prevent self-sowing, which is especially bad in cool climates. Shade or hot days in spring can make the flowering stems stretch so that they require staking. Basically pest-free, but occasionally is attacked by stalk borer. Will grow from bits of root, so be sure to remove all the root of unwanted seedlings. No need to cut back in late fall or early spring; foliage self-destructs neatly over winter.

NOTES: 'Alba' is white. 'Rosea' and 'Carnea' are pink.

'Grandiflora' has larger blooms. Persian cornflower (*C. dealbata*) is a 24- to 36-inch pink-flowering relative that blooms several weeks later than perennial bachelor's button. Growing conditions and care are the same.

'Mountain Blue' perennial bachelor's button

CHELONE OBLIQUA

Rose turtlehead

3'
2'

- Dense shade to full sun; must have continuous moisture or wet soil if in full sun
- Any moist soil, even wet, neutral to acid
- Average to excess moisture
- Deadheading not needed
- Divide every four to five years, running roots; needs pampering after moving
- Staking unnecessary
- Zones 4–9
- Snapdragon family

BLOOMS: Deep pink flowers on spikes resemble snapping-turtle heads. Late summer to fall.

SHAPE, SIZE, GROWTH RATE: Columnar, 2 to 6 feet tall and half as wide; spreads by shallow rhizomes into wide, dense colonies. Moderate growth rate.

ENVIRONMENTAL NOTES: Tolerates heavy clay and alkaline soils. Where summers are very hot, constant moisture is essential.

USES: Sturdy, vertical plant with medium-textured, deep green foliage. Good with mounded plants, finer- or coarser-textured plants, and species with rounded flowers: aster, black-eyed Susan, swamp milkweed, globe flower, meadow rue, queen-of-the-prairie, rodgersia, buttercup, Himalayan fleece flower, sedum, Japanese wax bell, daylily, dropwort, and maiden grass.

CARE: Apply 50 percent more fertilizer than for average perennials. To keep turtlehead in check near less aggressive plants, reduce the colony in spring each year. Divide every four to five years or topdress in late fall with 1 to 2 inches of compost to rejuvenate the clump. Seed germinates erratically unless first exposed to very high heat in moist soil. Basically pest-free. Powdery mildew may occur, particularly where soil is dry. Plant can be pinched several times

between midspring and midsummer to reduce height at flowering. Cut back in late fall or early spring.

NOTES: 'Bethelii' is more floriferous, deep rose-pink-flowered. 'Alba' is white-flowered, slow to grow.

White turtlehead (*C. glabra*) is similar but has white flowers with a red tinge. 'Black Ace' is white flowered with very dark stems and foliage. Pink turtlehead (*C. lyonii*) is similar.

Pink turtlehead

CIMICIFUGA RAMOSA

Fragrant bugbane

3-6'
3'

- Half sun to dense shade
- Moist acid soil with plentiful organic matter
- Constantly moist to soggy
- Deadheading not necessary
- Rarely needs division
- Zones 3–9, may need protection in Zone 3
- Buttercup family

BLOOMS: Sturdy, 3- to 4-foot white spikes in fall.

SHAPE, SIZE, GROWTH RATE: Three to 6 feet tall, half of that in leafless flower stalks and elegant spikes. Tallest where soil is constantly moist or wet; 2 to 3 feet wide. Clump-forming. Slow to moderate growth.

ENVIRONMENTAL NOTES: Prefers acid soil but tolerates neutral to slightly alkaline pH as well. Does not tolerate heat and drought. Avoid planting in full sun unless soil is constantly moist.

USES: Tall, ferny foliage, maroon in some varieties, is attractive with coarse, mounded plants such as hosta, rodgersia, heart-leaf brunnera, Japanese wax bell, celandine poppy, and Lenten rose. It blooms with toad lily, azure monkshood, and purple bush clover.

CARE: Apply 50 percent more fertilizer than for average perennials. Basically pest-free. Staking may be necessary where light is strongly one-directional. Stake individual stems. Cut down in late fall or early spring.

NOTES: 'Atropurpurea', 'Brunette',

and 'Hillside Black Beauty' begin the season with striking purple foliage, which may become green by summer.

Related species: black snake root (*C. racemosa*) has white spires high above ferny foliage in midsummer, 4 to 8 feet. Spreads quickly by underground runners and seed. Kamchatka bugbane (*C. simplex*) is studded with pearly white buds that tease from July until mid- to late fall, finally opening to ivory bottlebrushes after first frost. Clump-forming or slowly spreading by rhizomes, 3 to 5 feet.

Fragrant bugbane

'Brunette' bugbane

CLEMATIS HERACLEIFOLIA

Blue-bush clematis

3-4'

3'

- Shade to full sun
- Moist, well-drained soil with plenty of organic matter
- Average to constant moisture
- Deadhead to prolong bloom; branched flowers

'Wyevale' blue-bush clematis

- Rarely needs division, running roots
- Crutches or grow-through supports
- Zones 3–9
- Buttercup family

BLOOMS: Clusters of fragrant, sky blue or blue-violet flowers in late summer.

SHAPE, SIZE, GROWTH RATE: Bushy, 3 to 4 feet tall and half again as wide. Slow to become established but then spreading at moderate rate by underground rhizomes into sizable colonies.

ENVIRONMENTAL NOTES: Must have constantly moist soil if grown in full sun. Does not tolerate very hot summers or wet soil in winter. Tolerant of a wide pH range.

USES: Large, light green leaves and semisprawling habit lend themselves to sturdy, ferny or finer-textured companions such as bugbane, obedient plant, goatsbeard, and turtlehead.

CARE: Basically pest-free. Resistant or immune to the clematis wilt fungus that affects large-flowered vining clematis. Topdress with 1 to 2 inches of compost in late fall or very early spring to maintain the soil's organic content. Cut back in spring to encourage upright growth; if intended as a ground cover, only remove dead wood. May be staked, given the support of neighboring plants, or allowed to sprawl.

NOTES: 'Davidiana' has darker blue flowers; petals do not curl back on themselves as much as the species, so they appear larger. 'Wyevale' has small, dark blue flowers, is more lightly scented, and has finely divided foliage.

Other shrubby, late-blooming clematis include: Durand's clematis (*C. × durandii*), 3 to 5 feet tall, deep violet flowers from mid- to late summer. Zones 5–9. Solitary clematis (*C. integrifolia*), 2 to 3 feet tall and wide, with nodding bell flowers with twisted petals in violet, pink, blue or white. Early to midsummer. Zones 3–8.

COREOPSIS LANCEOLATA

Lanceleaf coreopsis

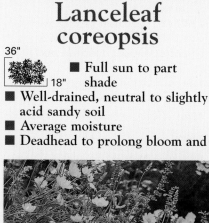

36"

18"

- Full sun to part shade
- Well-drained, neutral to slightly acid sandy soil
- Average moisture
- Deadhead to prolong bloom and prevent self-sowing; branched flower stems
- Small crutch supports
- Divide every two to three years to maintain vigor; offsets; easy to move
- Zones 3–9
- Aster family

BLOOMS: Early to midsummer, with repeat bloom if cut back before seeds set; golden to brassy-yellow 2-inch-wide daisies.

Tickseed (C. grandiflora) *is nearly identical to lanceleaf coreopsis. The main difference is that it blooms more prolifically.*

Finely textured threadleaf coreopsis (C. verticillata) *is covered in blooms from midsummer on. It grows 10 to 24 inches tall.*

SHAPE, SIZE, GROWTH RATE: Loosely columnar, 18 inches wide and 3 to 4 feet tall in bloom. Some cultivars are short (10 inches) and mounded. Most of the foliage is at the base of the plant. Very fast growth. Clump form spreads by offsets and seed.

ENVIRONMENTAL NOTES: Tolerates drought and alkaline soil. Does not tolerate wet soil in winter.

USES: Combines well with perennial salvia, ornamental mullein, and speedwell, or with ornamental grasses.

CARE: Cut back hard after first flowering to stimulate production of new flowers. Don't deadhead or cut back if seeds desired to attract birds. Basically pest-free. Four-lined plant bug can disfigure foliage beginning just before bloom. Powdery mildew or rust may develop, especially if the plants are not in full sun. May need staking, especially in rich, moist soil. Apply fertilizer at half the average rate to avoid soft, floppy growth. Cut to the ground in late fall or early spring.

CORYDALIS LUTEA

Yellow corydalis

1'
1½'

- Half sun to dense shade
- Moist, well-drained soil with plentiful organic matter; tolerates alkaline soil
- Average to constant moisture
- No need to deadhead
- Rarely needs division; hard to move
- Staking unnecessary
- Zones 5–10
- Bleeding heart family

BLOOMS: Butter-yellow flowers like tiny snapdragons from midspring to midsummer.

SHAPE, SIZE, GROWTH RATE: Mounded, 6 to 15 inches tall and wide. Fast growth. Spreads rapidly by reseeding where conditions are right.

ENVIRONMENTAL NOTES: Tolerates drought once established. Will take sun if soil is cool and constantly moist, but foliage and flower color fade. Doesn't do well in heat.

USES: Combines with hosta (particularly effective with gold-variegated cultivars) and yellow-flowered forms of barrenwort, Japanese wax bell, heart-leaf brunnera, or Solomon's seal.

CARE: Basically pest-free. No need to deadhead and would be quite a chore to do since so many flowers are borne so freely over so long a time on such a short plant. Self-sows but easily weeded out. Surprisingly, packaged seed is difficult to germinate. Best to collect fresh seed from an established planting, which will germinate readily the following spring if sown immediately after collection. Difficult to move except as seedling; may reestablish slowly.

NOTES: One of the best "unknown" shade plants. Often difficult to find at garden centers because it transplants with difficulty from seed flats into pots. It then does not present itself well, because its delicate stems are easily broken in handling and shifting of stock.

Blue corydalis (C. *flexuosa*) has smoky-blue flowers and blue-green foliage. It is striking in cool, rich, shaded areas. Unlike yellow corydalis, it goes dormant in summer.

Yellow corydalis

CROCOSMIA X CROCOSMIIFLORA

Crocosmia

1½'
1-1½'

- Full to half sun
- Well-drained, rich, moist soil; blooms best in clay soil
- Constantly moist, but does not tolerate wet soil and poor drainage
- Deadhead, multi-cluster
- Divide in spring every three years, runners from corm-like tubers
- May require staking in part shade, use individual braces
- Zones 5–9
- Iris family

BLOOMS: Lights up a midsummer border with glowing red-orange or yellow funnel-shaped flowers that line the arching tip of each stem.

SHAPE, SIZE, GROWTH RATE: Flaring, swordlike foliage makes a vase-shaped clump 18 to 30 inches tall and wide. Spreads by short rhizomes from gladiolus-like corms. Moderate rate.

ENVIRONMENTAL NOTES: Does not tolerate drought. Sometimes listed as hardy only to Zone 6, but winter losses in Zone 5 are probably a result of poor drainage or very young plants. Larger roots are hardier; cover new plants with a thick mulch for the first few winters until the plants are full size.

USES: Coreopsis and black-eyed Susan are complementary in form and add other hot colors to the scheme. Pearly everlasting, cool yellow-green patrinia, 'Silver King' artemisia, or the white form of globe thistle make the vase-shaped blue-green crocosmia jump out in contrast. Try a deep violet-blue delphinium for an arresting sight, or ornamental grasses to tone it down.

CARE: Slugs, snails, and mites may be a problem; if there is extensive damage to the foliage in spring or early summer, bloom will be reduced. Self-cleaning (spent flowers drop off). Clip off entire stem when last bud opens and finishes bloom.

NOTES: 'Vulcan' is deep red-orange and hardier than some varieties. 'Lucifer' is bright red and 12 to 24 inches taller than most. 'Jenny Bloom' is a yellow-flowered variety.

'Lucifer' crocosmia

DELPHINIUM ELATUM

Delphinium

3-6'
- **Full to half sun**
- **Moist, rich, well-drained soil**
- **Average to constant moisture**

3'

- **Deadhead to prolong flowering, standard spike**
- **Divide every three years; offsets**
- **Stake individual stems, tying in at 12-inch intervals**

'Blue Springs' delphinium

- Zones 3–7
- Buttercup family

BLOOMS: Tall wands with blue, violet, pink, white, or two-toned flowers. Early to midsummer.

SHAPE, SIZE, GROWTH RATE: An 18-inch mound of foliage in spring develops into a column 3 to 6 feet tall when it blooms. Clump-forming. Moderate growth rate.

ENVIRONMENTAL NOTES: Tolerant of a wide pH range. Does not tolerate wind, heat, drought, or poorly drained soil. Must have shade at midday.

USES: Combine with later-blooming tall plants: perennial sunflower, globe thistle, Joe-Pye weed, anise hyssop, fragrant bugbane, 'Lucifer' crocosmia, ornamental grasses, ironweed, or culver's root. In bloom, it complements queen of the meadow and meadow rue.

CARE: Apply 50 percent more fertilizer than for average perennials. Leaf spot, powdery mildew, and stem and crown rot are problems. Remove and destroy all discolored foliage, flowers, and stems. Avoid problems by not crowding plants. Thin the shoots on established plants in early spring; allow just five to seven shoots per clump. Apply preventive fungicide.

Divide delphinium every three years in early fall, and grow the new plant in beds that have not held delphiniums in the past several years. Slugs and snails can be a problem, as can stalk borer.

Staking is necessary except on the shortest cultivars. Remove entire flowering stalk when deadheading, cutting just above a large leaf low on that stem. New flowering shoots will develop from the stem. After second bloom, cut off flower stems. Water and fertilize. Wait for new basal shoots to emerge and old foliage to wither, then remove old stalks.

Grows from seed or stem cuttings taken in spring and rooted in water. Cut down in late fall and remove all foliage to reduce pest problems.

DENDRANTHEMA X GRANDIFLORUM

Chrysanthemum

2'
- **Full to half sun**
- **Moist, rich, well-drained soil**

2'

- **Average moisture**
- **Divide every two years in spring; offsets**
- **Crutches or grow-through supports for tall, unpinched plants**

'Lemon Blanket' chrysanthemum

- Zones 5–9
- Aster family

BLOOMS: Flowers come in many forms, including single and double daisies, and pompom. All colors except blue. Mid- to late summer and fall, varying by variety and maintenance practices.

SHAPE, SIZE, GROWTH RATE: Mounded to columnar plants, vary by variety from 12 to 48 inches. Fast growth rate.

ENVIRONMENTAL NOTES: Does not tolerate wet soil. Good in windy locations if soil moisture is high. Cold-hardiness affected by drainage; mums planted late in the season or in poorly drained soil are less likely to survive winter in Zones 5–6.

USES: Combines well with vertical plants, such as purple coneflower, crocosmia, gas plant, ironweed, and ornamental grasses.

CARE: Apply 50 percent more fertilizer than for average perennials. Pinch several times between midspring and midsummer for bushier, shorter, later-blooming plants. May be necessary to stake unpinched plants. If flowering stems develop in spring (warmer zones), pinch these back to encourage strong, leafy growth.

Aphids, Japanese beetles, mites, slugs, snails, and nematodes can be problems. Leaf spot, mildew, and rust infect older, crowded clumps. Rabbits, deer, and woodchucks graze on the flower buds. Cut back in early spring in Zones 5–6, or cover with airy mulch over winter if cut down in late fall. Divide every two years to keep clumps vigorous. Replant in new location in garden to prevent buildup of pests.

NOTES: Korean hybrids have vivid color and increased hardiness.

Montauk daisy (*Nipponanthemum nipponicum*) is a semievergreen woody perennial 24 to 36 inches tall with lustrous leaves and white daisies in fall. Zones 5–9. Do not pinch it in Zones 5–6; its bloom may be delayed beyond freeze date. Montauk daisy is virtually pest-free and tolerant of wind and salt.

DIANTHUS ALLWOODII

Allwood pinks

15"

15"

- Half to full sun
- Sandy soil with excellent drainage
- Average moisture; allow to dry down between waterings
- Deadhead to prolong bloom; branched flower stems
- Divide every two to three years; offsets
- Staking unnecessary
- Zones 4–8
- Carnation family

BLOOMS: Frilly miniature carnations in all colors and combinations except blue. Single, semidouble, and double-flowered forms. Late spring to early summer.
SHAPE, SIZE, GROWTH RATE: Mound of grassy foliage 10 to 15 inches tall and wide. Clump-forming. Fast to grow.
ENVIRONMENTAL NOTES: Does not tolerate wet soil or pH below 6. Tolerates heat and drought but not heat and high humidity.
USES: Combine pinks' grassy silvery or blue-green foliage with coarser front-of-the-border plants, such as perennial geranium, 'Silver Brocade' artemisia, coral bells, dwarf bearded iris, ornamental mullein, and perennial salvia. Blooms with perennial bachelor's button, 'May Queen' daisy, and gas plant.
CARE: Fertilize and water well throughout the growing season for repeat bloom in fall or late summer where nights are cool. Attracts rabbits. Leaf spot can be a problem, especially where soil is moist, humidity high, and air circulation poor. To propagate, pull off stem sections, each with a bit of woody basal tissue intact (stem cuttings with a "heel"), and root these in early fall. Cut back foliage in early spring, leaving intact the leafy base of woody stems.
NOTES: 'Doris' is salmon pink with a darker pink center. 'Ian' is rich red with black-red petal edge; may be hardy only to Zone 5.

Cottage pink *(D. plumarius)* is more cold-hardy (Zone 3) and blooms in yellow, white, and pink varieties. 'Mountain Mist' is rose-pink, mat-forming, and more tolerant of heat and humidity than many others. Cheddar pink *(D. gratianopolitanus)* and maiden pink *(D. deltoides)* are shorter, mat-forming pinks and more tolerant of summer heat and humidity. 'Bath's Pink' is a very floriferous pale pink. 'Red Maiden' is red-violet. 'Brilliancy' is nearly red (Zone 3).

Allwood pinks

DICENTRA SPECTABILIS

Bleeding heart

30"

36"

- Sun to shade
- Well-drained, sandy soil with plentiful organic matter
- Average to constant moisture
- No need to deadhead
- Rarely needs division; forked taproot; hard to move
- Staking unnecessary
- Zones 3–8
- Bleeding heart family

BLOOMS: Distinctive, large pink or white hearts dangle from arching stems. Mid- to late spring.
SHAPE, SIZE, GROWTH RATE: Large mound, 18 to 30 inches tall and 36 inches wide. Clump-forming with a deep root. Slow to grow.
ENVIRONMENTAL NOTES: Not tolerant of wet soil. If grown in full sun, dry soil, or great heat, summer dormancy begins earlier, leaving a large gap in the border.
USES: Coarse, smoky-green leaves mix well with coral bells, foam flower, monkshood, turtlehead, dropwort, astilbe, and hosta. Blooms with woodland phlox and heart-leaf brunnera. Pair with toad lily to hide the vacancy if bleeding heart goes dormant before fall.
CARE: Apply 50 percent more fertilizer than average. Basically pest-free. Resistant to rabbits, woodchucks, and deer. No need to cut back in late fall or early spring. Long-lived. Stems are self-cleaning. Self-sowing is minimal. Plant cannot flower again until it has experienced winter cold. Moving plants may break brittle roots; plants reestablish slowly.
NOTES: 'Pantaloons' is white.

Old-fashioned bleeding heart

Fringed bleeding hearts *(D. eximia* and *D. formosa)* are later blooming 18-inch-tall relatives with finely divided blue-green leaves. They usually do not go dormant and will repeat bloom if deadheaded; flowers are not heart-shaped. They prefer acid to neutral soil. Some varieties creep by rhizomes to form large patches; others stay in neat clumps. 'Luxuriant' has dark pink to cherry-red flowers. 'Snowflakes' is a dwarf white. 'Adrian Bloom' is rose-red and larger-flowered. Zones 3–9.

'Snowflakes' fringed bleeding heart

DICTAMNUS ALBUS

Gas plant

2-4'

3'

- Full sun to shade
- Moist, rich, well-drained soil
- Constantly moist
- Do not deadhead if seed stalks are desired for drying or for the garden; standard spike

- Rarely needs division; taproot
- Staking unnecessary
- Zones 3–8
- Citrus family

BLOOMS: Starry white or pale rose flowers open on tall spikes over shining, dark green foliage. An impressive sight in bloom or later when ripe brown seedpods open to form a wand of nut-brown stars. Midspring.

SHAPE, SIZE, GROWTH RATE: Sturdy, columnar plant 2 to 4 feet tall and almost as wide. Clump-forming. Slow to grow.

ENVIRONMENTAL NOTES: Does not tolerate dry soil, poor drainage, or hot nights.

USES: Excellent partner to peony in overall appearance, bloom, and longevity. Foliage color and texture contrast nicely with Siberian and Japanese irises, yellow or pink threadleaf coreopsis, globe thistle, daylily, and swordleaf inula.

CARE: Apply 50 percent more fertilizer than for average perennials. Basically pest-free.

If leaf-chewing damage is seen, look closely before taking action; gas plant is a host to larvae of black swallowtail and giant swallowtail butterflies. Move or divide in spring or early fall as necessary, or leave in place for a lifetime (it's not true that the plant will die if disturbed). Can be propagated by root cuttings. Seed is difficult to germinate and may require two full years of freeze-thaw cycles. Stems falling over mean the plant needs more water. Cut back in late fall or early spring.

NOTES: Sharp lemon fragrance of flowers and foliage is pleasant to some, disturbing to others. Use care in working around the plant on hot days; oil from the leaves on the skin reacts after exposure to sunlight to cause a burnlike rash. This oil escapes from the developing seedpods on hot days and can be ignited. It is said to burn quickly without damaging the plant, thus the common name gas plant. 'Purpureus' flowers pale rose with darker veins. Enchanting.

Gas plant

ECHINACEA PURPUREA

Purple coneflower

2-4'

2'

- Full to half sun
- Well-drained soil
- Average moisture
- Deadhead to prolong bloom into fall; branched flower stems

- Divide every four to five years in fall or spring to maintain vigor; offsets; easy to move
- Staking unnecessary
- Zones 3–9
- Aster family

BLOOMS: Daisylike rosy-pink or white flowers circle prominent central cones with an intriguing rusty hue. Petals curl back from cone as blooms age. Early to midsummer.

SHAPE, SIZE, GROWTH RATE: Columnar plant 2 to 4 feet tall and half as wide. Coarse-textured. Clump-forming. Fast growth rate.

ENVIRONMENTAL NOTES: Tolerates heat, humidity, drought, wind, and shade.

USES: Shape and texture works well with bear's breeches, ornamental grasses, Russian sage, queen of the meadow, blazing star, artemisia, obedient plant, culver's root, checkerbloom, and sedum.

CARE: Basically pest-free. Older, crowded clumps may develop stem dieback, a viral infection; remove

them. Self-sows; seedlings are variable in height, color, and flower size. Watch for especially nice homegrown varieties. Seeds attract birds; seed heads provide winter interest. Cut back in late fall or early spring.

NOTES: 'Magnus' has larger, darker pink flowers with a less pronounced central cone. Flower petals do not droop with maturity. 'Robert Bloom' has very large, dark pink petals; cone has a more pronounced rusty hue, 2 to 3 feet. 'White Lustre' and 'White Star' have ivory flowers with a sweet, light scent. Half the height of the species. Slow to grow.

Pale coneflower (E. angustifolia) is 2 to 3 feet tall. Its late-spring to early- summer flowers are paler pink than those of purple coneflower with long, wispy petals that hang and flutter. The flower stalks are less leafy and more flexible with the overall impression being that of pink badminton shuttlecocks swaying in the breeze. Zone 4.

Purple coneflower

ECHINOPS RITRO

Globe thistle

3-5'

2-3'

- Full to half sun
- Well-drained soil
- Average moisture
- Deadhead to prolong bloom
- Divide in spring; infrequent; offsets
- Staking unnecessary. May need grow-through supports in shade and rich soil
- Zones 3–9
- Aster family

BLOOMS: Spheres of steely blue buds in early summer, open to pale blue flowers in midsummer.

SHAPE, SIZE, GROWTH RATE: Strong, coarse column 3 to 5 feet tall. Fast growth. Clump-forming.

ENVIRONMENTAL NOTES: Flowers fade to pale blue in hot weather. Takes drought, heat, and shade.

USES: Coarse gray-green foliage and unique spherical flowers are attractive with ornamental grasses, crocosmia, speedwell, checker-bloom, obedient plant, daylily, daisy, perennial sunflower, and false sunflower.

CARE: Basically pest-free; occasional stalk borer. Painted Lady caterpillars may knit shoot tips together in spring but will be gone in time for plant to grow new foliage and bloom. Apply fertilizer at half the average rate for perennials. In lieu of deadheading, cut back flowering stems after first flush of bloom to promote new basal growth. Will rebloom in fall in cool, moist growing seasons. Self-sows. Do not deadhead all flowers if attracting birds is desired. Cut back in late fall.

NOTES: 'Taplow Blue' has large and steel-blue flowers. 'Veitch's Blue' is darker blue.

Russian globe thistle (*E. exaltatus*) is taller, to 8 feet. Silvery white flowers. Cut-leaf globe thistle (*E. tenuifolius*) has more finely divided foliage and bright blue flowers.

Globe thistle

EPIMEDIUM GRANDIFLORUM

Barrenwort

6-15"

15"

- Half to full shade
- Well-drained soil with plentiful organic matter
- Average moisture
- No need to deadhead
- Rarely requires division; offsets; easy to move
- Staking unnecessary
- Zones 4–9
- Barberry family

BLOOMS: Early spring. Pink or rose flowers are delicately winged and dangle on wiry stems, usually too low to the ground or close in among the foliage to be seen by the casual observer. New leaves are complementary, starting out bronze, expanding to green, and showing bronze again in fall and winter.

SHAPE, SIZE, GROWTH RATE: Low, wide colony of heart-shaped leaves on wiry stems, 6 to 15 inches tall and gradually growing wider. Slow to moderate spread.

ENVIRONMENTAL NOTES: Tolerates drought, dense shade, and competition from tree roots.

USES: This evergreen is good with other winter-interest shade plants: coral bells, foam flower, Lenten rose. Subtle two-tone foliage echoes pink-flowered bleeding heart, hybrid lobelia, tellima, lungwort, perennial geranium, dropwort flower buds, or 'Painter's Palette' tovara variegated leaves. Elegant with large blue-leaved hostas.

CARE: Basically pest-free. Root weevils may sometimes be a problem. Resistant to rabbits and browsing deer. Cut down previous year's foliage in late fall or late winter so that next year's flowers are more visible. No need to deadhead; new foliage expands to hide flowering stems. Rarely needs division. Divide as desired in spring or fall.

NOTES: 'Rose Queen', large crimson flowers; 'White Queen' blooms silver-white. 'Pierre's Purple' is taller with large purple blooms.

Foliage of red barrenwort (*E. × rubrum*) has rosy undertones and margins. New species are becoming available. Watch for taller species (*E. davidii* and *E. × omeiense*) and species with showier flowers (*E. brachyrrhizum*) which are being introduced from China and Korea.

Young's barrenwort** (E. × youngianum) **has deep crimson foliage in fall. 'Niveum' with white blooms and 'Roseum' with rose flowers are the most readily available cultivars.

EUPATORIUM COELESTINUM

Hardy ageratum

18-24"

24"

- Full sun to shade
- Well-drained soil with plentiful organic matter
- Average to constant moisture
- Deadhead to reduce self-seeding; branched flower stem
- Divide every four to five years; offsets; easy to move
- Staking unnecessary; pinch back if it grows floppy
- Zones 4–10
- Aster family

BLOOMS: Powder blue flowers open from late summer into fall.

SHAPE, SIZE, GROWTH RATE: Mounded, 18 to 24 inches tall; may grow much wider. Spreads by shallow white stolons below soil surface. Fast to very fast growth.

Hardy ageratum

Joe-Pye weed attracts butterflies; foliage and flowers have a vanilla scent.

ENVIRONMENTAL NOTES: Does not tolerate heat, wet soil, or poor drainage.

USES: Complements plants with vertical lines, such as obedient plant, speedwell, culver's root, blazing star, and iris. Blooms with perennial fountain grass and sedum.

CARE: Basically pest-free. Powdery mildew can be a problem. Spreads; dig out excess plants and seedlings annually to prevent it from overwhelming neighbors. Do not leave roots of significant size in place if trying to eliminate.

NOTES: May be found as *Conoclinium coelestinum*. 'Album', white flowers; 'Wayside', shorter, with larger flowers.

Joe-Pye weed (*E. purpureum* and *E. maculatum*) is mauve-flowered and reaches 7 feet by late summer. Give it full- to half-sun and moist to wet soil; stake in shade and high heat; attracts butterflies. 'Gateway', bronze stems; huge, light-colored blooms; 5 feet. 'Atropurpureum', reddish-purple stems; Zone 3.

EUPHORBIA POLYCHROMA

Cushion spurge

12-20"

24"

- Full to half sun
- Well-drained soil
- Average to dry
- Do not deadhead
- Divide every five to six years; offsets
- Staking unnecessary
- Zones 4–9
- Spurge (poinsettia) family

BLOOMS: Clusters of tiny flowers backed by showy, long-lasting chartreuse bracts top each stem in early to midspring.

SHAPE, SIZE, GROWTH RATE: Strongly mounded, 12 to 20 inches tall and a bit wider. Clump-forming. Slow to moderate growth rate.

ENVIRONMENTAL NOTES: Tolerant of heat, drought, wind, and alkaline soil. Does not tolerate high humidity, wet or poorly drained soil.

USES: Goes with bright pinks, red-violets, and purples of early tulips,

Cushion spurge often develops reddish orange fall color.

Myrtle spurge (E. myrsinites) is a better choice for humid Southern summers. It is a prolific self sower. Zones 5–9.

creeping phlox, dwarf bearded iris, and beard-tongue; complements peony foliage. Stems hide foliage of fading spring bulbs.

CARE: Basically pest-free. Resistant to rabbits, woodchucks, and deer. Sap repels moles and voles. Divide every five to six years to reduce crowding. Where summers are very hot, plant in half sun and divide more frequently. Can be propagated by tip cuttings in late spring or early summer. When cutting, take care to rinse skin of milky sap, which can cause a burnlike rash.

NOTES: 'Emerald Jade', 12 inches, reliable fall color. 'Purpurea', purple cast to the foliage.

Griffith's spurge (*E. griffithii*) is strongly columnar, sometimes invasive; 30 inches; Zones 5–9. 'Fireglow', flowers resemble glowing, then fading embers. 'Dixter', flowers are red fading to orange; foliage has purple undertones. Less vigorous spreader than 'Fireglow'.

FILIPENDULA VULGARIS

Dropwort

12-18" | 18"

- Sun to shade
- Most garden soils with plentiful organic matter; prefers neutral to slightly acid pH
- Constantly moist to wet or even soggy
- Deadhead to prolong bloom, keep the clump neat, and reduce self-sowing; branched flower stem
- Divide every five to six years in spring or fall; offsets; easy to move
- Grow-through support or crutches, if needed
- Zones 3–9
- Rose family

BLOOMS: Buds with a pink cast open to creamy white flowers in dense clusters at the tips of tall, nearly leafless stems. Late spring to early summer.

SHAPE, SIZE, GROWTH RATE: Mounded foliage 12 to 18 inches tall and wide. Flower stalks rise 3 feet tall. Clump-forming. Moderate growth rate.

ENVIRONMENTAL NOTES: Tolerates high humidity, wind, and alkaline soil. Tolerates heat, if given partial shade and constant moisture, and dry soil, where air is cool.

USES: Combines with everything.

CARE: Basically pest-free. May develop leaf spot or powdery mildew in dry soil. Cut back in early spring.

NOTES: 'Flore Pleno', double flowers; 'Kahome', a dwarf with pink blooms.

Dropwort before bloom

Queen-of-the-prairie (*F. rubra*) is 3 to 7 feet tall with coarse foliage and pink cotton-candy blooms in early to midsummer. Forms dense colonies in moist to soggy soil. Full to half sun. May require staking in hot summers or dry soil. Not invasive. 'Venusta' has deeper pink flowers. Meadowsweet (*F. ulmaria*) produces clouds of white flowers in early summer; forms dense colonies in moist to soggy soils; shade-tolerant, 3 to 5 feet tall. 'Aureo-variegata' has dark green leaves variegated with cream and yellow.

Queen-of-the-prairie

GAILLARDIA X GRANDIFLORA

Blanket flower

2-3' | 1½'

- Full sun
- Well-drained soil; prefers sandy soil with plentiful organic matter
- Average to constant moisture
- Deadhead for neatness; branched flower stems
- Divide every two to three years in spring; offsets; easy to move
- Stake tall types; grow-through or crutches
- Zones 2–10
- Aster family

BLOOMS: Large, daisies with scented, warm-red-brown centers; petals are yellow with red-orange bases or tips. Early to midsummer.

SHAPE, SIZE, GROWTH RATE: Loosely upright stems 24 to 36 inches tall over coarse gray-green foliage concentrated at base of stems. Dwarf varieties form 12-to-15-inch-tall and wide mounds. Clump-forming; spreads by short,

running roots. Very fast growth rate.

ENVIRONMENTAL NOTES: Tolerates heat, drought, and wind. Does not tolerate wet or poorly drained soil.

USES: Coarse foliage and warm-colored flowers blend with yellow yarrow, threadleaf coreopsis, blackberry lily, crocosmia, daylily, ornamental grasses, and patrinia.

CARE: Basically pest-free. May develop crown rot where soil is wet, particularly in winter. Stake tall types or allow to sprawl; flowering stems will turn upright. The plant will have a shorter, broader presence in the garden.

Blooms continuously into fall even without deadheading. But seed heads detract from the flowers and make the plant look ragged. Allow some seed to set to promote self-sown replacements of this short-lived hybrid.

Can be propagated by root cuttings in spring. Grows easily from seed. No need to cut back in late fall or early spring; stems decompose quickly over winter. An airy mulch of twigs over the crown prevents deterioration of the crown over

winter in areas with heavy snows.

NOTES: 'Goblin' is 9 to 15 inches tall with petals that are mostly red, tipped yellow. 'Baby Cole' has a wide red zone on petals; it grows less than 12 inches tall. 'Burgundy' is a full-sized variety with red petals. Seed from named varieties do not grow true; seedlings may vary in height and flower color.

Blanket flower

GAURA LINDHEIMERI

White gaura

2-5'

2-3'

- Full to half sun
- Well-drained soil with plentiful organic matter

- Average to low moisture
- Deadhead occasionally to keep new flower stalks developing; multicluster
- Divide every two to three years or less often; offsets
- Staking unnecessary
- Zones 5–9
  - Evening primrose family

BLOOMS: White flowers like miniature butterflies dance on wiry, nearly leafless stems. Buds are pink; flowers are white, turning pink with age. Midsummer into fall. Will produce at least a few new flowers continuously, even if not deadheaded. Bloom commences earlier in regions with very warm springs.

SHAPE, SIZE, GROWTH RATE: An airy column 2 to 5 feet tall, sometimes taller in warm areas, 2 to 3 feet wide. Clump-forming. Fast growth.

ENVIRONMENTAL NOTES: Tolerates drought, heat, humidity, and wind but not wet soil. Blooms may fall off in midsummer if nights are hot.

USES: Not a star on its own, but a good complement to spring-blooming perennials with clean, dark green or blue-green summer foliage such as false indigo, pinks, gas plant, peony, blue oat grass, beard-tongue, and soapwort. Pretty in bloom with balloon flower and tall phlox.

CARE: Basically pest-free. Cut to the ground in late fall or early spring. May be divided every two to three years, or allow seedlings to replace parents. Allow some seed to set if naturalized self-sowing desired.

NOTES: 'Pink Cloud' has light pink flowers and very sturdy stems. 'Crimson Butterflies' has reddish foliage and stems; dwarf, 18 to 24 inches. 'Whirling Butterflies' is a dwarf form, 18 to 24 inches.

White gaura

GERANIUM SANGUINEUM

Bloody cranesbill

1-1½'

2'

- Half sun
- Well-drained soil
- Average to constant moisture
- No need to deadhead
- Divide every five to six years to renew vigor; running; easy to move
- Staking unnecessary

- Zones 3–8
- Geranium family

BLOOMS: 1-inch-wide red-violet, pink, or white flowers stud the plant surface from mid- to late spring. May rebloom.

SHAPE, SIZE, GROWTH RATE: 12 to 18 inches tall, 24 inches wide, spreading wider at moderate to fast rate. Clump-forming.

ENVIRONMENTAL NOTES: Tolerates shade, drought, heat, and a wide pH range. It's the only common cranesbill that tolerates full sun. Does not do well in poorly drained or wet soils.

USES: Good companion for almost any perennial. Effective with columnar- and vase-shaped plants that bloom in yellows or cool colors.

CARE: Basically pest-free. Leaf spot can be a problem. Cut back hard to remove infected foliage. Keep soil moist until plant grows back. Shear plant after first bloom for fresh foliage and reduced self-sowing. Self-sows widely. Cut back in early spring if desired or if leaf spot appeared the previous year.

Bloody cranesbill

Armenian geranium (G. psilostemon) holds its deep red-violet flowers above the foliage; 3 feet; Zones 4–8.

Big-root geranium (G. macrorrhizum) is semi-evergreen, grows to 18 inches; fragrant foliage. Zones 4–8.

Ornamental grasses

1-9'

- Full sun
- Well-drained, prefers neutral to slightly alkaline soil
1-4'
- Average to constant moisture
- Do not deadhead
- Divide every four to five years in early spring to control size of clump; offsets; easy to move
- Staking unnecessary
- Zone varies
- Grass family

BLOOMS: Silver, rose, or white plumes depending on species. Foliage may take on bronze, purple, or tawny cast.

SHAPE, SIZE, GROWTH RATE: Mounded to columnar to vase-shaped, up to 9 feet tall in bloom, 1½ to 4 feet wide. Clump-forming. Moderate growth rate.

ENVIRONMENTAL NOTES: Tolerates wind, heat, humidity, and salt. Some species take shade, wet soil, or drought.

USES: Combine with other grasses or plant with coarser, shorter and mounded plants that also supply fall and winter interest such as black-eyed Susan, sedum, false indigo, or catmint. Underplant small species with spring- and summer-flowering bulbs. Attract birds.

CARE: Generally pest-free. Voles may eat plant crowns in some winters. Cut back in early spring. Ease the job by tying up the grass before cutting; use a chainsaw, hedge trimmer, or loppers. Silver grass 'Variegatus' may require staking with a large, strong hoop.

NOTES: Maiden grass (*Miscanthus sinensis*): 'Strictus' and 'Zebrinus' are sturdy, upright variegated forms; Zones 4–9. 'Adagio' is a dwarf, 3 feet tall and wide; blooms in early fall, narrow, tan plumes. 'Silver Feather' has silvery plumes in early fall. 'Morning Light' is 4 feet tall and 3 feet wide with very narrow, white-striped foliage and plumes that are first red, then tan.

Feather reed grass (*Calamagrostis acutiflora*) has early summer blooms, and forms a narrow clump with spirelike seed heads, 4 to 5 feet tall, 18 inches wide. 'Karl Foerster', more upright, with dramatic seed heads. Tolerates half shade. Zones 5–9.

Sheep's fescue (*Festuca ovina*), a cool-season grass, is 8 inches tall. 'Elijah Blue' and other blue-foliaged varieties are striking. Wheatlike seed heads develop to 18 inches in late spring and should be removed shortly afterward to keep the plants neat and prevent self-sowing. Shear to 3 to 4 inches in early spring and comb to remove dead blades. Fast growth. Intolerant of wet or poorly drained soil.

Purple moor grass (*Molinia caerulea*) blooms in June with see-through, airy spangles on wiry stems 4 to 5 feet above the arching foliage. Seed heads sparkle like a mist over yellow-orange foliage, 7 to 8 feet. Zones 4–9.

Hakone grass (Hakonechloa macra), 1½ feet tall, clump-forming, half sun to shade, rich, moist soil. Slow-growing. No bloom. Avoid heat and drought. Zones 5–8.

Feather reed grass

Blue oat grass (Helictotrichon sempervirens), 2–3 feet tall and wide, semievergreen, blooms only in southern part of its range, needs dry soil and excellent drainage; does poorly in humidity. Zones 4–8.

Northern sea oats (Chasmanthium latifolium) 2–4 feet by 1–2 feet; clump-forming; shade-tolerant; self sows. Zones 4–8.

'Gracillimus' is a fine-textured maiden grass.

Perennial fountain grass (Pennisetum alopecuroides), 3–4 feet tall and wide, silvery-pink plumes in late summer; heat- and drought-tolerant. Clump-forming. Self sows. Zones 5–9.

HELIANTHUS X MULTIFLORUS

Perennial sunflower

3-6'
3-4'

- Full sun
- Moist, well-drained soil with plentiful organic matter
- Constant to average moisture
- Deadhead to prolong bloom; branched flower stems
- Divide every three years in fall or spring; offsets
- Taller varieties may need staking, individual braces or long crutches
- Zones 4–8
- Aster family

BLOOMS: Bright yellow flowers 3 inches wide, single or fully double. Late summer to fall.

SHAPE, SIZE, GROWTH RATE: Sturdy column, 3 to 6 feet tall, half as wide, gradually becoming wider. Moderate to fast growth rate.

ENVIRONMENTAL NOTES: Tolerates half sun, heavy clay, and a wide pH range.

USES: Combine this coarse, columnar plant with mounded perennials, fine-textured ornamental grasses, and spike flowers such as black-eyed Susan, pearly everlasting, chrysanthemum, fountain grass, anise hyssop, azure monkshood, blazing star, cardinal flower, and Russian sage.

CARE: Apply 50 percent more fertilizer than for average perennials. Powdery mildew can be a problem in dry soil and in older clumps. Maintain constant moisture and divide every three years in fall or spring to facilitate air circulation within the clump. Slugs, aphids, and four-lined plant bugs can sometimes be problems; occasional stalk borer. Foliage dies back as flowering finishes; not a problem but a natural cycle. Can be pinched several times from midspring to early summer to restrict height. Do not deadhead if you desire seeds to attract birds. Double-flowered forms are seedless.

NOTES: 'Morning Sun' is a single-flowered variety, 5 feet. 'Loddon Gold' is fully double, 4 to 5 feet. 'Capenoch Star' is a lighter yellow, 3 to 4 feet.

'Triomphe de Gand' perennial sunflower reaches 4 feet tall.

HELIOPSIS HELIANTHOIDES SCABRA

False sunflower

3-4'
2'

- Full sun
- Well-drained soil with plentiful organic matter
- Constant to average moisture
- Deadhead to prolong bloom; branched flower stems
- Divide every three to four years to maintain vigor and full bloom; offsets
- Staking unnecessary
- Zones 4–9
- Aster family

BLOOMS: 3-inch brassy or clear yellow flowers early to late summer. Has a very long bloom period.

SHAPE, SIZE, GROWTH RATE: Coarse column, 3 to 4 feet tall, 2 feet wide. Clump. Fast growth rate.

ENVIRONMENTAL NOTES: Tolerates drought, half sun, a wide pH range, and heavy clay soil. Needs some midday shade in very hot regions. Does not tolerate wet or poorly drained soil.

USES: Coarse-textured columnar plant is a good backdrop or partner for shorter, mounded, and finer-textured perennials such as lavender, catmint, peony, and perennial salvia. Impressive in bloom near spike-flowered bear's breeches, blazing star, culver's root, or speedwell.

CARE: Powdery mildew may be a problem; increase water and fertilizer. Aphids, leafhoppers, and four-lined plant bugs can disfigure the foliage. Do not deadhead if seed production for birds is important. Self-sows; seedlings will be variable and probably inferior to named varieties in height and bloom. If stems flop outward, improve drainage and increase early-season water and fertilizer in future years. Cut back in late fall or early spring.

NOTES: 'Summer Sun' is a double-flowered soft-yellow variety that grows 3 feet tall.

'Summer Sun' false sunflower

HELLEBORUS ORIENTALIS

Lenten rose

1-1½'

1½-3'

- Half sun to shade
- Moist, well-drained soil with plentiful organic matter
- Constant to average moisture
- Deadheading not required
- Rarely needs division
- Staking unnecessary
- Zones 4–9
- Buttercup family

BLOOMS: Saucer-shaped cream, green, purple, or pink flowers 2 to 3 inches wide in nodding or out-facing clusters. Blooms may be multihued, such as pink petals spotted purple or flushed green. Opening buds are borne upward over several days as stems elongate to 12 inches or more. Colorful for weeks. Late winter to early spring.

SHAPE, SIZE, GROWTH RATE: Coarse, lustrous, deep green foliage 12 to 18 inches tall and 18 to 30 inches wide. Clump. Slow-growing.

ENVIRONMENTAL NOTES: Tolerates alkaline soil. Tolerates and even thrives in full sun in cool climates if provided ample water and shaded during winter. May need extra protection in Zones 4–5 if snow cover is not reliable. Does not tolerate wet or poorly drained soil. Performs poorly in windy areas and warm spring weather.

USES: Complements ferny, pale foliage and columnar shapes: red baneberry, astilbe, bugbane, all bleeding hearts, barrenwort, dropwort, cardinal flower, Jacob's ladder, Solomon's seal, lady's mantle, big root geranium, hakone grass, variegated hosta, lungwort, rockcress, and foam flower.

CARE: Slugs, snails, and root weevils may be a problem. Leaf spot may occur, especially if soil is very heavy or acid. Remove infected foliage and apply fungicide if sanitary measures do not help. Resistant to rabbits and browsing deer. Foliage is evergreen. Cut back old growth before plant blooms.

Apply 50 percent more fertilizer than for average perennials as new foliage emerges. If you divide plants, do so in spring while in bloom, before root growth begins for season. May not bloom the following year. Self-sows. Natural hybrids are often pleasing. Watch for and transplant seedlings from among flowering stems before shaded out by expanding foliage.

NOTES: Most Lenten roses sold in the U.S. are mixed seedlings with unknown color unless purchased in bloom.

Lenten rose

HEMEROCALLIS HYBRIDS

Daylily

1-6'

2-3'

- Full to half sun
- Well-drained soil with plentiful organic matter
- Average moisture
- Deadhead to keep plant neat; tip cluster
- Divide every four to five years or when flowering falls off; offsets; easy to move
- Staking unnecessary
- Zones 3–9
- Lily family

BLOOMS: Wide range of flower colors—near-white, yellow, red, and violet—and flower forms, including single, double, trumpet, and bell. Some bloom in late spring; others peak in early, mid-, or late summer. Repeating bloomers have several flushes each year.

SHAPE, SIZE, GROWTH RATE: 1 to 2 feet tall and wide mounds. Flowers may skim the top of the foliage or rise several feet; heights range from 1 to 6 feet. Most are clump-forming with moderate growth rate. Some spread very fast.

ENVIRONMENTAL NOTES: Stands up to heat, drought, shade, salt, foot traffic, competition from tree roots, flooding, and wind. Adversities diminish flower quality and quantity.

USES: Complements most other perennials.

CARE: Fertilize regularly but not heavily. Leaf diseases can cause foliage to decline in summer. Slugs, snails, and late-spring frost damage make plants vulnerable to disease. Attracts rabbits, woodchucks, muskrats, and deer. Snap off spent flowers at their base. Remove stems when last bud opens. No need to cut back in late fall or early spring except for sanitation if leaf diseases are a problem.

NOTES: Late spring to early summer bloom: 'Siloam Purple Plum', 'Lullaby Baby'; early summer: 'Astolat', 'Coral'; mid- to late summer: 'Cherry Cheeks', 'August Flame', 'September Gold'; repeat bloom: 'Daring Dilemma'; extended bloom (until evening): 'Happy Returns'; fragrant; 'Hyperion'. Miniatures (small flowers on full-sized plants): 'Golden Chimes'.

Daylily (H. flava)

'Stella de Oro' is a short repeat bloomer, beginning in early summer.

HEUCHERA SANGUINEA

Coral bells

6-18"

12"

- Shade to full sun
- Well-drained soil with plentiful organic matter
- Average to constant moisture
- Deadhead to prolong bloom; multicluster flower
- Divide every two to three years to maintain vigor; offsets
- Staking unnecessary
- Zones 3–8
- Rockfoil family

BLOOMS: Tiny red, pink, or white bells on wiry stems in late spring.
SHAPE, SIZE, GROWTH RATE: Mound of evergreen foliage, 6 to 12 inches tall and wide with flowers rising above the mound another 6 to 12 inches. Clump-forming. Moderate growth rate.
ENVIRONMENTAL NOTES: Tolerates competition with tree roots if topdressed with 1 to 2 inches of compost every fall.
USES: Pairs well with low and mat-forming evergreens.
CARE: Root weevils can be serious. Cut away old or damaged foliage in early spring.

NOTES: Varieties with green foliage: 'Firebird', deep red flowers, 18 inches in bloom; 'Chatterbox', large pink flowers, 18 to 24 inches. Purple-leaf coral bells (*H. micrantha* and *H. americana* hybrids), Zones 4–9: 'Pewter Veil', silvery cast to leaf edges and areas between veins, green-white flowers, 18 inches; 'Chocolate Ruffles', foliage deep maroon, white flowers, 24 inches.
× *Heucherella* (coral bells crossed with foam flower), Zones 4–9: 'Quicksilver', white flowers, bronze foliage with silver variegation, 18 inches; 'Rosemary Bloom', coral, 18 to 24 inches.

Coral bells

'Alba Rosalie' × *Heucherella*

Purple leaf coral bells take heat.

HIBISCUS MOSCHEUTOS

Hardy hibiscus

3-5'

3'

- Full sun
- Rich soil with plentiful organic matter
- Constantly moist to soggy
- Divide every seven to 10 years; forked taproot; easy to move
- Zones 5–9
- Hollyhock family

BLOOMS: Huge crepe-paper pink, red, and white disks, often with a dark eye. Mid- to late summer.
SHAPE, SIZE, GROWTH RATE: Rock-solid mounded plant 3 to 5 feet tall, 3 feet wide. Moderate growth rate.
ENVIRONMENTAL NOTES: Tolerates heat (requires heat to develop good bloom) and a wide pH range. Does not tolerate drought. Wind doesn't bother plant but shreds flowers.
USES: A coarse mound to contrast with vertical and finer textures and smaller flowers such

as Siberian and Japanese iris, blazing star, fleece flower, Joe-Pye weed, swamp milkweed, turtlehead, tufted hair grass, cardinal flower, great blue lobelia, obedient plant, checkerbloom, and culver's root. Attracts hummingbirds.
CARE: Japanese beetles and caterpillars can damage foliage. Apply 50 percent more fertilizer than for average perennials. Use a saw to separate sections of woody root. Easy to grow from seed; blooms in its first year. Cut back in late fall or early spring. Stems are very stiff but not woody. Shoots rise from the old stem bases and roots, emerging late in spring.
NOTES: 'Southern Belle', red, pink or white, 4 to 6 feet tall. 'Kopper King', maroon foliage, pink flowers, 3 to 4 feet tall and wide. Zone 4.
Scarlet rose mallow (*H. coccineus*) has deeply lobed leaves, 6 to 8 feet tall and half as wide. Red flowers are large but funnel-form rather than flat. Zones 7–9.

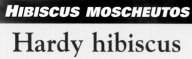

White 'Disco Belle' hardy hibiscus

Hostas

½-2½' ½-3'

- Half sun to shade
- Well-drained neutral to slightly acid soil with plentiful organic matter
- Constant to average moisture
- Deadhead, removing entire flower stalk; standard spike
- Divide every seven to eight years; offsets; easy to move
- Staking unnecessary
- Zones 3–9
- Lily family

BLOOMS: Lilac or white bells hang from tall stalks in midsummer. Most hostas are grown for the foliage, which is blue, green, or variegated with cream or gold. Leaves are round or oval. Leaf surface may be thick and distinctly quilted.

SHAPE, SIZE, GROWTH RATE: Mound of coarse foliage, 24 to 30 inches tall. Flowering stalks may add 12 or more inches. Clump-forming, 2 to 3 feet wide, slowly spreading wider.

ENVIRONMENTAL NOTES: Tolerates sun if temperatures are cool and water plentiful. Tolerates alkaline soil. Intolerant of drought.

USES: Plant with mat-forming perennials or species with strong vertical lines or finer foliage: red baneberry, Japanese anemone, goatsbeard, astilbe, Serbian bellflower, turtlehead, bugbane, yellow corydalis, fringed bleeding heart, barrenwort, blue flax, creeping forget-me-not, woodland phlox, Jacob's ladder, Solomon's seal, meadow rue, tovara, and toad lily. Attracts hummingbirds; some species are fragrant.

CARE: Slugs, snails, rabbits, and deer can ruin the foliage. Voles and root weevils may eat the roots. Hostas with thick leaves and quilted surfaces are resistant to slugs and snails. Under trees that host heavy insect populations, sooty mold may grow on dripping insect excrement and disfigure leaves. Rinse foliage regularly, and plant smooth-leaved hostas, which are more self-cleaning than quilted types. The big, blue-leaved hostas are unusual in

producing more flowers if the season is long and first blooms are removed before seed is set. Do not deadhead if sturdy, persistent seed stalks are part of your winter garden design. Cut down plants and topdress with compost in late fall or very early spring. Fertilize regularly.

NOTES: Blue-leaf siebold hostas (*H. sieboldiana*) include 'Elegans', large leaves with amber fall color. 'Frances Williams', large leaves irregularly edged in creamy yellow. 'Great Expectations', blue edges, leaf center streaked cream, gold, and green.

There are many hosta species, ranging from diminutive 8-inch dwarf hosta (*H. venusta*) to giants such as the hybrid 'Sum and Substance', with puckered gold foliage 3 feet tall. Most are clump-forming, but there are creeping ground covers such as blunt hosta (*H. decorata*). Here is a sampler of other hosta species:

H. nigrescens varieties such as 'Krossa Regal'. Lance-shaped gray-green foliage. Upright, vase-shaped clump. Flower stalks rise 3 to 6 feet, and attractive seedpods persist through winter.

H. nakaiana varieties such as 'Golden Tiara'. Small, heart-shaped leaves edged in gold. Clumps are very dense, 8 to 12 inches tall, with purple flowers barely taller. Heavy blooming. Excellent for edging and ground cover.

Blue hosta (*H. ventricosa*) has large, smooth, shiny foliage and dark purple flowers. 'Aureo-marginata' has wide, irregular, creamy white edges.

Fragrant hosta (*H. plantaginea*) has large, heavily scented white flowers like flaring trumpets in late summer, after most other hostas have bloomed; 18 inches tall in leaf, 24 inches in bloom. Clumps are 24 inches wide, slowly spreading wider. Foliage is light green and thin, more prone to slug and snail damage than others here. Hybrids include 'Sugar and Cream', with fragrant, pale lilac flowers and quilted, slug-resistant foliage. Zones 4–9.

'Big Daddy'

'Krossa Regal'

Hosta flower portrait

'Sugar and Cream' fragrant hosta

IBERIS SEMPERVIRENS

Evergreen candytuft

10"
18"

- Full to half sun
- Well-drained, sandy soil with plentiful organic matter
- Average moisture
- Shear to deadhead to promote dense evergreen growth
- Divide every four to five years in spring or fall; running
- Staking unnecessary
- Zones 3–8
- Mustard family

BLOOMS: White flowers in 1-inch thimble-shaped clusters cover the plant in midspring.

SHAPE, SIZE, GROWTH RATE: Mat of fine-textured, dark evergreen foliage, 6 to 10 inches tall and 12 to 18 inches wide or more. Moderate growth rate.

ENVIRONMENTAL NOTES: Heat tolerant. Does not tolerate wet or poorly drained soil. If snow cover is not reliable in cold regions, foliage will desiccate and branches die back.

USES: Complements coarse-textured, mounded, or vertical plants and other species with winter interest such as Himalayan fleece flower, rockcress, coral bells, iris, thrift, and sheep's fescue. Blooms with columbine and catmint.

CARE: Basically pest-free. Clubroot may infest older plantings in poor soil. Destroy plants and do not plant mustard family species there for several years. Evergreen, so do not cut plants back in fall. In windy, open areas in Zones 3–5, cover with twigs or evergreen boughs during winter to prevent dehydration and dieback. Divide every four to five years in spring or fall and add organic matter when replanting.

NOTES: May bloom lightly in a long, cool autumn. 'Alexander's White' is especially dense and free-flowering.

Evergreen candytuft

INULA ENSIFOLIA

Sword-leaf inula

2'
2'

- Full sun
- Well-drained soil with plentiful organic matter
- Average moisture
- Divide every four to five years in spring or fall to maintain vigor; offsets; easy to move
- Zones 4–8
- Aster family

BLOOMS: Long-lasting yellow daisies with narrow petals in early summer.

SHAPE, SIZE, GROWTH RATE: Dense mound, 18 to 24 inches tall and wide. Clump; spreads by short, shallow rhizomes. Moderate growth rate.

ENVIRONMENTAL NOTES: Wind-tolerant. Does not tolerate high heat and humidity or wet, poorly drained soil.

USES: A fine-textured mound combines well with coarse, columnar, and vase-shaped plants such as butterfly weed, yarrow, blackberry lily, clustered bellflower, perennial salvia, blue oat grass, blazing star, many-flowered sunflower, and speedwell. Attracts butterflies.

CARE: Basically pest-free. Shear after flowering for repeat bloom. Cut to the ground in early spring. Add organic matter to the soil when replanting.

NOTES: 'Compacta' is less than a foot tall, 12 to 18 inches wide.

'Sunray' sword-leaf inula

IRIS HYBRIDS

Iris

½–3' 1½'

- Full sun
- Well-drained, sandy soil
- Average to low moisture
- Deadhead after bloom to hasten development of new, clean foliage; branched flower stems
- Divide every four years in early to midsummer; multiple eyes on rhizomes; easy to move
- Stake tall varieties with individual braces
- Zones 3–9
- Iris family

BLOOMS: Every imaginable color and color combination except true red. Blooms in spring. Shortest varieties bloom earlier in spring than taller types but all peak by early summer.

SHAPE, SIZE, GROWTH RATE: Swordlike leaves grow 6 to 18 inches tall, depending on variety, and 18 inches wide. Flower stalks rise 6 to 40 inches high. Spreads by stout rhizomes on or just under the surface. Fast growth.

ENVIRONMENTAL NOTES: Tolerates heat and alkaline soil. Does not do well in wet soil or shade. Tall varieties of bearded iris do not stand up to wind.

USES: Combine with mounded and finer-textured plants such as dwarf aster, yarrow, golden marguerite, Carpathian harebell, threadleaf coreopsis, pinks, cushion spurge, sword-leaf inula, perennial flax, catmint, and black-eyed Susan. Attracts hummingbirds; fragrant.

CARE: Iris borers are a problem, chewing between the folds of the foliage and down into the root. Iris soft rot follows the borer damage and can devastate iris plantings. Control the borers with thorough cleanup of all old foliage every fall and spring; apply insecticide as necessary in spring when borer damage is first noticed; divide regularly in early summer when borer grubs in the roots are easily destroyed.

Stake tall varieties in windy locations, where soil is very rich, or if plants were recently transplanted. Use braces for individual stems. Stake after dividing or moving.

NOTES: 'Argentea Variegata' sweet iris (*I. pallida*) has a wide white stripe on each leaf. Foliage is dramatic, clean throughout summer, and resistant to borer damage; 12 inches; lilac flowers to 18 inches. 'Aurea Variegata' has a wide creamy yellow stripe up each leaf. Zones 5–8.

Siberian iris (*I. sibirica*) forms a narrow, grassy clump 30 to 40 inches tall. Attractive in and out of bloom. Seedpods can be allowed to develop and left in place for winter interest. Tolerant of wet and even soggy soils and part shade. Stands up well in windy areas. Resistant to soft rot and so less endangered by borer damage. Blooms with the latest bearded iris. 'Caesar's Brother' is a classic, dark blue-violet. 'Butter and Sugar' is a white and yellow bicolor. Zones 3–9.

Japanese iris (*I. ensata*) is similar to Siberian iris; 24 to 30 inches in leaf; flower stems may rise 12 inches higher. Wide flowers that open almost flat; later-blooming than Siberian iris. Tolerant of wet soil during the growing season but not during the winter. Requires neutral to acid soil. 'White Heron', large white flowers. Zones 4–9.

Louisiana hybrids have taller, wider foliage than Siberian and Japanese iris but are otherwise similar in appearance and use. Unique among irises in having near-red varieties. Zones 5–10.

Bearded iris

Siberian iris

Japanese iris

'Argentea Variegata' sweet iris

KIRENGESHOMA PALMATA

Japanese wax bell

2-3'
3'

- Half sun to shade
- Rich neutral to slightly acid soil with plentiful organic matter
- Constant to average moisture
- Deadhead if desired; branched flower stem
- Rarely needs division
- Staking unnecessary
- Zones 5–8
- Rockfoil family

Japanese wax bell

BLOOMS: Large, creamy yellow bells hang from stem tips in fall.
SHAPE, SIZE, GROWTH RATE: Coarse, shrublike mound of maple-leaf-shaped foliage, 2 to 3 feet tall and a bit wider. Clump. Slow growth.

ENVIRONMENTAL NOTES: Does not tolerate heat or drought. Takes very heavy soil and most other conditions if moisture needs met.
USES: Combines well with finer-textured, shorter, and more columnar plants such as bugbane, astilbe, goatsbeard, meadow rue, yellow corydalis, cardinal flower, and globe flower. Blooms with azure monkshood and toadlily.
CARE: Basically pest-free. Foliage may scorch in sun or dry soil. In Zones 5–6, frost usually ends the bloom period so seed is rarely set. Cut back in late fall or early spring. Young plants can be mistaken for maple seedlings; take care in weeding.

LAVANDULA ANGUSTIFOLIA

English lavender

- Full sun
- Well-drained, sandy soil

1-3'
1-3'

- Average moisture
- Deadheading not needed
- Rarely needs division
- Staking unnecessary
- Zones 5–9
- Mint family

English lavender

BLOOMS: Tiny fragrant purple or gray-white flowers in dense spikes; early summer.
SHAPE, SIZE, GROWTH RATE: Mound of gray foliage, 1 to 3 feet tall and wide, depending on type and growing conditions. Clump. Slow to moderate growth.
ENVIRONMENTAL NOTES: Tolerates drought, heat, and wind, but not high humidity, wet soil, or poor drainage.

USES: Attractive with coarser textures, taller plants, and blue-green and maroon foliage colors: bear's breeches, blackberry lily, purple-leaf coral bells, fountain grass, sunflower, bee balm, and ornamental mullein. Blooms with butterfly weed and daylily.
CARE: Four-lined plant bug may disfigure foliage. Cut back to vigorous wood in early spring. Shear after bloom to promote density and repeat bloom. Propagate by seed, layering, or tip cuttings in spring.
NOTES: 'Alba', white flowers, small plant. 'Munstead', blue-violet. 'Hidcote Blue', violet. 'Lavender Lady', dwarf, repeat bloom.

LESPEDEZA THUNBERGII

Thunberg bush clover

3-5'
2'

- Full to half sun
- Deep, well-drained soil
- Average moisture
- Deadhead to prolong bloom; multicluster
- Rarely needs division
- Staking unnecessary
- Zones 4–9
- Pea family

BLOOMS: Tiny, pealike pink, rose, or white flowers along tops of stems in fall.
SHAPE, SIZE, GROWTH RATE: Strongly columnar until bloom season, when stems lean out and plant becomes vase-shaped, 3 to 5 feet tall and 2 feet wide. Clump. Slow to moderate growth rate.

'White Fountain' bush clover

ENVIRONMENTAL NOTES: Tolerates drought, heat, wind and a wide pH range.
USES: Excellent with ornamental grasses and shorter, coarser, mounded plants.
CARE: Basically pest-free. Leafhoppers may disfigure foliage in spring and early summer. Cut to the ground or to live wood, in early spring. Blooms later if cut to the ground. To divide, approach the plant with work boots and sturdy tools, as you would an established shrub. Use a saw to separate rooted sections.
NOTES: 'Gibraltar' is a floriferous pink-flowered form, arching nearly to the ground when in bloom.

LEUCANTHEMUM X SUPERBUM

Shasta daisy

1-3'
- Full to half sun
- Well-drained soil
- Average moisture
1½'
- Deadhead to prolong bloom and prevent excessive self-sowing; branched flower stem
- Divide every two to three years in fall or spring to keep clump vigorous; offsets; easy to move
- Grow-through stakes for taller varieties
- Zones 4–9
- Aster family

BLOOMS: Classic white daisies with yellow centers in early summer.
SHAPE, SIZE, GROWTH RATE: Columnar in bloom, reverts to a basal rosette when cut back after bloom. Size in bloom varies by variety, from 10 to 36 inches tall and 18 inches wide. Expands by offsets. Fast to very fast.

ENVIRONMENTAL NOTES: Tolerates alkaline soil.
USES: Excellent with spiky flowers such as speedwell, Himalayan fleece flower, 'Purple Rain' salvia, ornamental mullein, and checkerbloom, and other flower shapes such as yarrow, bellflowers, delphinium, globe thistle, bee balm, and lavender.
CARE: Apply 50 percent more fertilizer than for average perennials. Some varieties repeat-bloom if cut back before seed is set. Aphids can be a problem. Four-lined plant bug can disfigure foliage just before bloom. Nematodes, crown or stem rot, wilt, and viral infections occur on older plantings and in wet soil. Discard oldest, central portion of plant to help control pest buildup—you'll still have too many divisions from each clump; occasional stalk borer. Resistant to browsing deer. Easy to grow from seed.
NOTES: Some references list this plant as *Chrysanthemum × superbum*. 'Alaska' and 'Becky' are 24 to 30 inches, with sturdy stems and extended bloom period if deadheaded. 'Becky' performs well in hot, humid summers. 'Silver Princess' is a 9-inch-tall dwarf. 'Marconi' and 'Aglaia' are double-flowered forms; best in half sun. 'Aglaia' is 18 inches, 'Marconi' up to 30 inches. Related *L. vulgare* 'May Queen' is hardier (Zone 3) and blooms in midspring; reblooms after being cut back; 18 to 24 inches. Its stems are thin and can be beaten down by rain.

Shasta daisy

LIATRIS SPICATA

Blazing star

3-5'
- Full sun
- Rich soil with plentiful organic matter
1-1½'
- Constantly moist to soggy
- Deadhead to prolong bloom and keep plants neat; top-down spike
- Divide in fall or spring every four to five years; offsets; easy to move
- Stake if needed; individual braces
- Zones 3–9
- Aster family

BLOOMS: Tall, stiff bottlebrushes of purple or white. Topmost flowers open first, so stalk blooms in a burnt-match pattern. Midsummer.
SHAPE, SIZE, GROWTH RATE: Columnar, with grassy foliage, 3 to 5 feet tall, 12 to 18 inches wide. Clump. Moderate to slow growth.
ENVIRONMENTAL NOTES: Tolerates wind and heat. Avoid drought; it causes reduced bloom and early dormancy.
USES: Excellent with low and mounded plants, grassy foliage, and daisy-shaped flowers such as pearly everlasting, golden marguerite, pink threadleaf coreopsis, purple coneflower, perennial geranium, false sunflower, daylily, bee balm, patrinia, meadow rue, hardy hibiscus, Siberian iris, tufted hair grass, and Shasta daisy.
CARE: Basically pest-free. Voles may eat the cormlike roots during winter. Clip flowering stem above the larger, basal foliage as blooming finishes. Self-sows. Tall varieties need staking in average to dry soil. Stake individual stems or increase water. Cut back in late fall or early spring.
NOTES: 'Kobold', purple, 18 to 24 inches. 'August Glory', blue-violet, 3 to 4 feet.
Rough gayfeather (*L. aspera*) has flowers in tufts along the tall wands, 3 to 6 feet tall. May need support; stake individual stems. Kansas gayfeather (*L. pycnostachya*) is similar in bloom time but is suited to dry soil, 5 feet. Older clumps often need support. Stake individual stems and divide every other year.

Blazing star

Rough gayfeather

LINUM PERENNE

Perennial flax

- Full to half sun
- Well-drained, sandy soil

Perennial flax

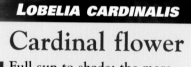

1½-2'
1'

- Average moisture
- Deadhead to prolong bloom; multicluster
- Division not needed; hard to move
- Staking unnecessary
- Zones 5–8
- Flax family

BLOOMS: 1-inch-diameter violet, blue-violet, or white flowers in late spring and early summer.
SHAPE, SIZE, GROWTH RATE: Vase-shaped plant, 18 to 24 inches tall and a bit wider. Clump. Very fast.
ENVIRONMENTAL NOTES: Tolerates heat, drought, wide pH range. Intolerant of wet or poorly drained soil.

USES: Filler among earlier- and later-blooming dense-foliaged plants.
CARE: Basically pest-free. Cut back each branch when more seedpods are forming below the open flowers than there are buds developing above them. Self-sows. Short-lived. Difficult to divide and transplant after first year; may not reestablish. Can move seedlings. Cut back in late fall or early spring.
NOTES: 'Alba', white flowers. Golden flax (*L. flavum*), butter-yellow flowers on 18-inch stems, longer-lived than blue flax; 'Compactum', 6 to 9 inches. 'Heavenly Blue' (*L. narbonense*), blue flowers with white eye, 12 to 18 inches.

LOBELIA CARDINALIS

Cardinal flower

- Full sun to shade; the more sun, the more water required

Cardinal flower

3'
1'

- Rich, moist soil with plentiful organic matter
- Constantly moist to wet
- Deadhead to prolong bloom; standard spike
- Divide every three or four years; offsets
- Staking unnecessary
- Zones 3–8
- Lobelia family

BLOOMS: Brilliant red flowers on tall spikes in mid- to late summer.
SHAPE, SIZE, GROWTH RATE: Narrow habit of 3- to 4-foot flowering stems; 12- to 18-inch-wide clump. Fast growth.

ENVIRONMENTAL NOTES: Does not tolerate drought. Grows in bogs but languishes in ordinary soil with average water.
USES: Vertical accent among mounded plants.
CARE: Basically pest-free. Cut back in late fall or early spring.
NOTES: Great blue lobelia (*L. siphilitica*), more tolerant of dry soil, 2 to 3 feet tall, midsummer blooms in shades of blue, short-lived but self-sows, Zones 4–8. Hybrid lobelia (*L. × speciosa*): 2 to 3 feet tall, 1 foot wide, red-violet, fuchsia, pink, white, and blue-violet flowers, long bloom season, Zones 5–8.

MONARDA DIDYMA

Bee balm

- Half to full sun; the more sun, the more water required

'Garden Scarlet' bee balm

1½-4'
3'

- Well-drained neutral to slightly acid soil with plentiful organic matter
- Constantly moist to wet
- Deadhead to prolong bloom
- Divide every two to three years; offsets; easy to move
- Grow-through supports if needed
- Zones 4–8
- Mint family

BLOOMS: Lilac, pink, red, and white flowers in early summer.
SHAPE, SIZE, GROWTH RATE: Columnar plant, 3 to 6 feet tall. Half that width in two to three years, spreading wider. Fast growth.

ENVIRONMENTAL NOTES: Doesn't tolerate drought or high humidity.
USES: Combines well with Joe-Pye weed, maiden grass, goatsbeard, astilbe, masterwort, turtlehead, bugbane, dropwort, and hibiscus.
CARE: Powdery mildew is a serious problem. Grow only resistant varieties. Four-lined plant bug disfigures foliage. Invasive; divide or remove excess plants frequently. Grows from root cuttings, so dig up all roots. Cut back in late winter or early spring.
NOTES: Resistant to mildew: 'Jacob Cline', red, 3 to 5 feet; 'Violet Queen', 3 to 4 feet; 'Marshall's Delight', 3 to 4 feet and 'Petite Delight', 20 inches, lilac.

MYOSOTIS SCORPIOIDES

True forget-me-not

6-8"

8"

- ■ Half sun to shade; full sun only if soil is wet or boggy
- ■ Well-drained soil, plentiful organic matter
- ■ Constantly moist to wet
- ■ Deadheading not needed
- ■ Divide every three to four years; offsets
- ■ Staking unnecessary
- ■ Zones 3–8
- ■ Forget-me-not family

BLOOMS: Carpets of tiny, baby-blue flowers with yellow centers in mid- to late spring.

SHAPE, SIZE, GROWTH RATE: Ground-hugging. Very fast growth; spreads 18 inches or more per year.

ENVIRONMENTAL NOTES: Tolerates some foot traffic. Does not do well in heat or drought.

USES: As an edging for the front of gardens; as a pretty spacer under and between moisture-loving half-sun plants that also require good air circulation such as bee balm, tall phlox, globe flower, azure monkshood, meadowsweet, and queen-of-the-prairie.

CARE: Basically pest-free. Crown rot may kill patches in mid- to late summer if grown where summers are very hot or soil is dry. Cut back as desired each spring to keep within bounds. Remove oldest portion of a colony every three to four years; mix compost into the soil and allow remaining plants to recolonize that renewed soil.

NOTES: Will repeat bloom in late summer if air is cool and moisture abundant.

Woodland forget-me-not (M. sylvatica)

NEPETA X FAASSENII

Catmint

1½-2'

2'

- ■ Full to half sun
- ■ Well-drained soil
- ■ Average moisture
- ■ Deadhead by shearing after spring bloom
- ■ Divide every five to six years to renew vigor; offsets; easy to move
- ■ Stake with crutches
- ■ Zones 4–8
- ■ Mint family

BLOOMS: Blue-violet spike flowers against scented gray-green foliage in midspring to early summer.

SHAPE, SIZE, GROWTH RATE: Mounded, fine-textured plant 18 to 24 inches tall and wide. Clump. Very fast growth.

ENVIRONMENTAL NOTES: Tolerant of drought, heat, wind, and some foot traffic. Does not perform well in regions with very hot, humid summers.

USES: Good partner for coarser-textured, taller plants with vertical lines: bearded iris, blackberry lily, obedient plant, yarrow, purple coneflower, many-flowered sunflower and balloon flower. Attracts butterflies and beneficial insects; fragrant.

CARE: Basically pest-free. Four-lined plant bug may disfigure foliage. Cut back in early spring. Can be cut to the ground in late fall, but if left in place, the frost-flattened stems and decomposing foliage act as a weed-smothering mulch during the off-season.

NOTES: *N. × faassenii* is a sterile hybrid, sometimes confused at garden centers with look-alike relatives such as *N. mussinii*, which is a prolific self-sower. If self-sowing occurs, deadhead to reduce the number of volunteers, and consider replacing the plants. 'Blue Wonder' has deeper blue-violet flowers and is only 12 to 15 inches tall and wide. 'Walker's Low' is even more compact.

Siberian catmint, Six-Hills Giant (*N. sibirica*), is later-blooming, 2 to 3 feet tall. If deadheaded, it will bloom from early to late summer. Upright, but may tend to flop toward the end of the season. Stake with crutches in spring, pinch for bushiness in spring; or cut back hard after it collapses and let it regenerate in the cool of late summer and fall. Self-sows. Zones 3–8.

Catmint

OENOTHERA FRUTICOSA

Sundrops

1½-2'

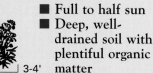

2'

- Full to half sun
- Well-drained soil
- Average to constant moisture
- Divide and remove central

clump portion every three to four years; offsets; easy to move
- Deadhead to prolong bloom
- Staking unnecessary
- Zones 4–9
- Evening primrose family

BLOOMS: Yellow flowers from early to midsummer.

SHAPE, SIZE, GROWTH RATE: Sturdy, upright spreader, 18 to 24 inches tall and as wide in one to two years, spreading wider. Very fast growth.

ENVIRONMENTAL NOTES: Tolerates wind, heat, and drought.

USES: Combine with other vigorous spreaders of various heights and textures in a naturalized garden: Siberian catmint, 'Fire King' yarrow, golden marguerite, bloody cranesbill, perennial ageratum, daylily, and tall phlox.

CARE: Basically pest-free. Cut back hard after flowering falls off to encourage new vegetative growth. Cut back

hard in late fall. Basal rosettes are evergreen, maroon in cold weather, and form an attractive off-season ground cover. To control the spread, dig out excess plants annually to prevent this assertive plant from overwhelming its neighbors. Remove and discard the oldest, central portion of the clump every three to four years. Mix a generous amount of compost into that area and allow outlying plants to recolonize the renewed soil.

NOTES: 'Fireworks' has red buds and reddish stems, eye-catching with the yellow flowers.

Ozark sundrops (*O. missouriensis*) is a sprawling plant with large, long-lasting lemon-yellow flowers. Give it rich, moist, well-drained soil in full sun. Less than 12 inches tall but stems spread 18 inches. Zones 4–8.

Showy evening primrose (*O. speciosa*) has enchanting daytime blooms that open light pink and fade to rose, 18 inches. Spreads deep and wide with underground runners and can become a terrible nuisance in rich soil. Zones 5–8.

Sundrops

PAEONIA LACTIFLORA HYBRIDS

Peony

3-4'

3-4'

- Full to half sun
- Deep, well-drained soil with plentiful organic matter
- Average moisture
- Deadhead to reduce weight on stems; dead petals can host botrytis infection; branched flower stem
- Divide in fall every eight to

10 years to renew the plant and soil; multiple eyes
- Stake with grow-through support or hoop in early spring
- Zones 4–7
- Peony family

BLOOMS: Late spring to early summer, these plants present large flowers that may be single, double, or one of many intermediate forms in white, pink, red, lilac, and bicolors.

SHAPE, SIZE, GROWTH RATE: Medium- to coarse-textured mound, 3 to 4 feet tall and round. Clump. Slow growth.

ENVIRONMENTAL NOTES: Tolerant of wide pH range. Not worth growing in lean, dry soil. Intolerant of wind—has been bred for large flowers that are almost too heavy for its stems and need support.

USES: A workhorse in the border, its long-lasting foliage is background, fill, and support for many later-blooming perennials such as meadow rue, bush clematis,

Armenian cranesbill, Russian sage, balloon flower, culver's root, Japanese anemone, crocosmia, and blanket flower.

CARE: Botrytis infection is common; good sanitation is required to prevent the disease's spread and eventual decline of the plant. Dark spots on leaves, purple-brown streaks on stems, and small, dried, unopened flower buds are sites of infections. Remove all discolored foliage as you see it, and clean up all peony foliage in late fall to avoid infecting new shoots as they emerge in spring. Check roots and discard any that are distorted or soft.

Fertilizer is most important in spring as shoots are emerging. Deadheading cannot extend bloom or encourage production of new flowers; peonies will not flower until after plants have been chilled to below 40° F for several months. For this reason, they do not bloom satisfactorily in regions with very warm winters.

NOTES: Hundreds of beautiful varieties are available.

Peony

PAPAVER ORIENTALE

Oriental poppy

1½-3'
2'

- Full sun
- Well-drained soil with plentiful organic matter
- Average moisture
- Deadhead to keep the planting neat, or allow seedpods to develop for dried decorations
- Rarely needs division; forked taproot; hard to move
- Staking unnecessary
- Zones 2–7
- Poppy family

BLOOMS: Red, orange, pink, or white flowers open in mid- to late spring and break hearts when they finish blooming a short time later.

SHAPE, SIZE, GROWTH RATE: Flower stems range in height from 18 to 36 inches depending on variety and growing conditions. Moderate to fast growth rate.

ENVIRONMENTAL NOTES: Does not tolerate high wind or wet soil.

USES: Accent color where late-emerging perennials will cover its fading foliage. Pair with Japanese anemone, hibiscus, balloon flower, hardy ageratum, Joe-Pye weed, Russian sage, or butterfly weed.

CARE: Basically pest-free. Deadheading will not prolong bloom or stimulate a second flowering; flower formation requires a warm-season dormancy, then a period of chilling. Thus Oriental poppies do not bloom reliably in areas with very warm winters.

Foliage begins growth in mid- to late summer and persists through winter. Do not cut back in late fall. Leaves resume growth in early spring and are already dying back by early summer to enter a short summer dormancy. Foliage of established poppies can be cut back after bloom or allowed to die back naturally.

To propagate or to control the size of a planting, dig the fleshy taproots after flowering. Watch for wilting after moving. Plants will grow from root cuttings as well as from bits of roots left behind in digging. Removing an old clump can involve several seasons of digging out surviving roots.

NOTES: Poppies require good drainage, especially during winter. Plant with bog-tolerant Joe-Pye weed and hibiscus only in well-drained sites.

Oriental poppy

PATRINIA SCABIOSIFOLIA

Patrinia

3-6'
2'

- Full to half sun
- Well-drained soil with plentiful organic matter
- Average to constant moisture
- Do not deadhead in the first year
- Divide every four to five years to maintain vigor; offsets
- Staking unnecessary
- Zones 5–9
- Valerian family

BLOOMS: Visually airy, flat-topped, yellow-green flower clusters look like a tight grouping of chartreuse Queen Anne's lace. Mid- to late summer.

SHAPE, SIZE, GROWTH RATE: Flowers on sturdy stems, 4 to 6 feet tall, 2 feet wide. Clump, spreads by short stolons. Moderate growth rate.

ENVIRONMENTAL NOTES: Tolerates heat, humidity, drought, and wind. Does not tolerate wet soil in winter.

USES: Useful wherever a reminder of cool spring green is needed during summer's heat. Combine with perennials having dense flowers in hot or cool colors such as blanket flower, speedwell, Montauk daisy, ironweed, flame grass, many-flowered sunflower, hardy hibiscus, or cardinal flower. Attracts butterflies and beneficial insects.

CARE: Basically pest-free. Deadheading may prolong flowering but doesn't improve the plant's appearance. Developing seedpods carry on color and ruin the post-bloom, similar to the way lady's mantle blossoms transform subtly to seed. After observing patrinia's change for yourself, decide whether to deadhead in future years. Cut back in late fall or early spring.

NOTES: 'Nagoya', 3 feet tall, 18 inches wide. Don't be fooled by its springtime appearance. The 12- to 18-inch mound of basal leaves is very different in appearance from the feathery stem leaves. Flowering stems arise from established roots, so outer edges of a clump and new transplants may not flower.

Patrinia

PENSTEMON DIGITALIS 'HUSKER RED'

'Husker Red' penstemon

2-3½'

1½'

- Full to half sun
- Well-drained soil
- Average moisture
- Deadhead to prolong

'Husker Red' penstemon

bloom, finally removing entire flower stalk, or do not deadhead at all to enjoy the maroon stems and seedpods
- Divide every four to five years to maintain vigor; offsets; easy to move
- Staking unnecessary
- Zones 3–8
- Snapdragon family

BLOOMS: Cool white flowers with open mouths arrayed along tall maroon stems in late spring to early summer.

SHAPE, SIZE, GROWTH RATE: Erect stems 24 to 40 inches tall, 12- to 18-inch-wide clump, spreads at a moderate rate.

ENVIRONMENTAL NOTES: Tolerates heat and wind. Foliage may fade to bronze or green in summer heat. Does not tolerate wet soil in winter.

USES: Combine with gray, bright green, and tan foliage plants: 'Silver King' artemisia, pearly everlasting, Japanese iris, dropwort, cranesbill, feather reed grass, fountain grass, catmint, or peony. Blooms with early daylilies. Pair penstemon's

dark stems with a pink daylily or pink-flowered hardy hibiscus. Attracts hummingbirds.

CARE: Basically pest-free. Leaf spot or nematodes may trouble older clumps. Self-sows. Seedlings are variable but worth watching—many green-leaf volunteers from this dark-foliage parent. Cut back in late fall or early spring. Well-grown plants can be sturdy and attractive through the winter. Seed heads dry well and would be used in dry arrangements if they didn't have such an unpleasant smell.

NOTES: Penstemon hybrids have been treasured for a long time in English and European gardens. These North American natives are just coming home in varieties such as 'Prairie Dusk' and 'Sour Grapes', with blue-violet flowers on stems 18 to 24 inches. Long-blooming if deadheaded. Zones 4–8.

Common beard-tongue (*P. barbatus*), with tubular scarlet flowers, is very attractive to hummingbirds, 18 to 30 inches, Zones 3–7.

PEROVSKIA ATRIPLICIFOLIA

Russian sage

3-4'

3-4'

- Full sun
- Well-drained, lean soil, preferably sandy or gravelly
- Average to low moisture

Russian sage

- May be deadheaded but bloom period is very long regardless
- Rarely needs division
- May require staking in rich loam or moisture-retentive clay; use grow-through support or crutches
- Zones 3–9
- Mint family

BLOOMS: Tiny purple flowers flock the fragrant gray stems in mid- to late summer.

SHAPE, SIZE, GROWTH RATE: A shrub with small, lacy gray-green leaves, 3 to 4 feet tall and wide. Spreads by natural layering. Moderate growth rate.

ENVIRONMENTAL NOTES: Tolerates heat, drought,

alkaline soil, and wind, but not shade or poorly drained soil.

USES: This plant's airy gray-green foliage and whitish stems soften the harsh shadows that summer sun creates on coarse-foliage plants. It's like putting on sunglasses to take in Russian sage alongside many-flowered sunflower, Montauk daisy, purple coneflower, queen-of-the-prairie, bee balm, showy sedum, and tall phlox.

CARE: Basically pest-free. Fertilize at half the average rate. May need a protective winter mulch around branch bases in Zones 3–4 if snow cover is not reliable. Cut last year's branches to their base in early spring for upright new growth and better flowering. Propagate any time by cutting through and transplanting layered branches or taking tip cuttings in summer.

NOTES: Varieties 'Longin' and 'Blue Spire' are deeper violet and more upright than the species.

PHLOX PANICULATA

Garden phlox

3-3½'

1½-2'

- Half to full sun
- Well-drained soil with plentiful organic matter
- Average to continuous moisture
- Deadhead to prolong bloom; branched flower stems
- Divide clumps every three to four years; offsets
- Stake tall varieties with grow-through or individual braces
- Zones 4–8
- Phlox family

BLOOMS: White, pink, magenta, lilac, or two-color flowers in mid- to late summer.

SHAPE, SIZE, GROWTH RATE: 36 to 40 inches tall, 18 to 24 inches wide. Clump. Fast to very fast rate.

ENVIRONMENTAL NOTES: Tolerates wind and a wide pH range but not drought, extreme heat, and high humidity.

USES: Plant with balloon flower, speedwell, lobelia, turtlehead, checkerbloom, or bush clematis.

CARE: Problems can include powdery mildew, spider mites, and nematodes. Thin stems in spring to five or six per clump. Remove any discolored foliage, stems, or flowers. Cut to ground and remove tall phlox foliage in late fall. Discard centers after division; replant young sections.

Apply 50 percent more fertilizer than for average perennials. If stems flop, thin clumps and increase water and fertilizer next spring. Self-sows; seedlings often inferior in color or susceptible to disease.

Garden phlox

Creeping phlox (P. subulata) *is 6 inches tall, 2 feet wide, and blooms in early to midspring. Zones 3–9.*

Woodland phlox (P. divaricata) *grows well in shade; 12–15 inches tall, 12 inches wide; blooms in late spring. Zones 4–9.*

PHYSOSTEGIA VIRGINIANA

Obedient plant

2-4'

1-2'

- Full to half sun
- Most soils with plentiful organic matter
- Average to continuous moisture
- Deadhead to prolong bloom; standard spike
- Divide every two to three years to restrict the spread; offsets; hard to move
- Stake plants in shade; grow-through supports
- Zones 3–9
- Mint family

BLOOMS: Spiky pink flowers in late summer or white spikes in midsummer.

SHAPE, SIZE, GROWTH RATE: Columnar plant, 2 to 4 feet tall and half as wide. Stolons spread underground. Very fast growth.

ENVIRONMENTAL NOTES: Tolerates shade, but flowering is much reduced and may require staking. Does not tolerate drought.

USES: Vertical accent near mounded forms. Plant with cranesbill, catmint, Japanese anemone, chrysanthemum, Serbian bellflower, hardy ageratum, tufted hair grass, fountain grass, or prairie dropseed.

CARE: Basically pest-free. Four-lined plant bug may disfigure foliage. Very aggressive spreader. May be pinched several times before midsummer to reduce height. Cut to the ground in late fall or early spring. Watch for wilting after moving.

NOTES: 'Summer Snow', white, earlier to bloom, 24 inches. 'Vivid', deep pink, 18 to 24 inches. 'Variegata', pink flowers, striking cream borders on leaf, much slower growth rate, 3 feet. 'Miss Manners', white, 24 inches tall and 2–3 feet wide, much less aggressive.

Common name comes from characteristic of individual flowers on the spike to stay obediently in position when pushed left or right.

Obedient plant

PLATYCODON GRANDIFLORUS

Balloon flower

36"

18"

- Half to full sun
- Well-drained soil
- Average moisture

- Deadhead to prolong bloom; multicluster
- Divide in spring or fall; infrequent; root divisions; hard to move
- Stake individual stems
- Zones 4–9
- Bellflower family

BLOOMS: Blue buds like expanding balloons enlarge and open into cupped five-pointed stars of deep blue-violet, white, or pink. Early to midsummer.

SHAPE, SIZE, GROWTH RATE: Columnar to vase-shaped, 24 to 36 inches. Clump. Slow to moderate growth rate.

ENVIRONMENTAL NOTES: Tolerates drought and heat.

USES: The coarse texture and vertical profile of balloon flowers combines well with perennials of finer texture and mounded form, such as artemisia, yellow yarrow, catmint, pearly everlasting, blue flax, or perennial ageratum. Good contrast with daisylike flowers: golden marguerite, daisy, sword-leaf inula, and black-eyed Susan.

CARE: Basically pest-free. Slugs, snails, and rabbits may take their toll on the foliage. Slow to emerge in spring; be patient. Surround with early bulbs. Tallest forms and plants in shade and in very hot regions may need staking. Propagate by cuttings of pencil-thick side roots from the main taproot. Self-sows; seedlings quite variable. It's possible to delay bloom by pinching all or some of the stems in early summer. Rarely needs dividing. Cut back in late fall or early spring.

NOTES: 'Mariesii', dwarf, 18 to 24 inches. 'Shell Pink', 18 to 24 inches. 'Sentimental Blue', hybrid variety less than 12 inches tall.

Balloon flower

POLEMONIUM CAERULEUM

Jacob's ladder

2'

1'

- Half to full sun
- Most soils with plentiful organic matter
- Average moisture

- Deadhead to prolong bloom or reduce self-sowing; branched flower stems
- Divide every three to four years in fall or spring to maintain vigor and free blooming; offsets; easy to move
- Staking may be necessary; crutches or individual stem support
- Zones 3–8
- Phlox family

BLOOMS: Blue-violet or white flowers clustered at stem tips in mid- to late spring.

SHAPE, SIZE, GROWTH RATE: Clump with upright-arching stems to 24 inches and half as wide. Moderate to fast growth rate.

ENVIRONMENTAL NOTES: Tolerates shade and alkaline soil. Does not do well in heat, humidity, or drought. Provide continuous moisture and good drainage for plants in full sun. Flowers are faded and more fleeting in sun.

USES: Fine-textured foliage and upright-arching shape is good with coarse-mounded hosta, celandine poppy, fringe cups, lady's mantle, big-root cranesbill, lungwort, and globe flower.

CARE: Basically pest-free. Rabbits may browse. Can be cut back hard as flowering falls off to encourage all new foliage. No need to cut back in fall or spring; foliage decomposes rapidly over winter.

NOTES: 'Brise D'Anjou' has neat, cream-edged leaves. May be reluctant to bloom, but the foliage is so delightful you won't mind.

Leafy Jacob's ladder (*P. foliosissimum*) is taller and later to bloom, 30 inches. Attractive with 'Moonshine' yarrow and coreopsis.

Jacob's ladder

POLYGONATUM BIFLORUM

Small Solomon's seal

2-3'

1-2'

- Half sun to shade
- Most soils with plentiful organic matter
- Average to continuous moisture
- Do not deadhead; does not prolong bloom or stimulate new bloom but ruins the plant's profile
- Divide every five to six years in fall or spring; offsets; easy to move
- Staking unnecessary
- Zones 4–9
- Lily family

BLOOMS: Narrow creamy bells hang in pairs along arching stems, followed by blueberry-like berries. Mid- to late spring.

SHAPE, SIZE, GROWTH RATE: Arching columns, with one-directional lean toward strongest light; 18 to 36 inches tall and 12 to 24 inches wide, spreading wider. Moderate growth rate.

ENVIRONMENTAL NOTES: Tolerates drought and poor drainage. Does not do well in very hot summers and is likely to go dormant early.

USES: Upright-arching form contrasts with mounded hosta, fringe cups, lungwort, cranesbill, purple-leaf coral bells, heart-leaf brunnera, and the bleeding hearts.

CARE: Basically pest-free. Slugs and snails may disfigure foliage. Foliage may scorch in heat, drought, or full sun. No need to cut back in fall or spring; foliage and stems decompose quickly in winter.

NOTES: Look for indentations on the stout, running rhizome where previous years' stems were attached, like a wax-stamped seal; they're the origin of the common name and are a distinguishing characteristic between this plant and various species called false Solomon's seal.

Great Solomon's seal (P. commutatum) may reach 6 feet. Its foliage turns apricot in fall, so the plant becomes a stately, glowing shrub in the shade garden. Zones 3–8. Foliage of variegated Solomon's seal (P. odoratum 'Variegatum') is delicately outlined in ivory; 12 to 24 inches tall and wide. Zones 4–9.

Variegated Solomon's seal

POLYGONUM AFFINE

Himalayan fleece flower

9"

12"

- Full to half sun
- Most soils with plentiful organic matter
- Continuously moist to soggy
- Deadhead in midsummer to prolong bloom; standard spike
- Divide every four to five years in fall or spring; running; easy to move
- Staking not required
- Zones 4–8
- Knotweed family

BLOOMS: Pink or red flower buds on spikes become white as they mature. Long blooming period, so red- and white-flowering spikes are mixed across the same plant. Early to midsummer.

SHAPE, SIZE, GROWTH RATE: Coarse mat of overlapping leaves and stolons, 2 to 3 inches deep. Flower stalks 6 to 9 inches.

Spreading. Moderate to fast growth.

ENVIRONMENTAL NOTES: Tolerates some foot traffic and shade. Does not tolerate drought or high heat.

USES: As an edging or a spacer between larger plants, or where its persistent chocolate-brown winter foliage will add interest to the winter scene. Plant near thyme, thrift, soapwort, candytuft, or bigroot cranesbill.

CARE: Basically pest-free. Divide every four to five years in fall or spring to restrict the spread and promote vigor and free-flowering. Can be mowed to deadhead.

NOTES: 'Superbum' produces pink flowers that age to red. 'Dimity' is more compact and flower spikes rarely top 6 inches.

Snakeweed, or bistort (P. bistorta) forms a dense, spreading mound of large leaves in difficult, wet, or heavy soil; 12 to 24 inches tall. Variety 'Superbum' produces large pink poker flowers 1 to 2 feet above the foliage over a long season. Zones 4–8. Requires continuously moist or wet soil if in full sun.

Mountain fleece (P. amplexicaule) is a spreading mound 4 feet tall with coarse foliage and thin red or pink poker flowers from early to late summer. Good in heavy and poorly drained soils. 'Firetail' has bright red flower spikes up to 6 inches tall. Zones 4–8.

Himalayan fleece flower

PULMONARIA SACCHARATA

Lungwort

1-1½'

1½'

- Half sun to shade
- Well-drained soil with plentiful organic matter
- Average moisture
- No need to deadhead
- Rarely requires division; running; easy to move
- Staking unnecessary
- Zones 3–8
- Borage family

BLOOMS: Early to midspring show of bells that dangle from 18-inch stems. Pink buds mature to blue flowers.

SHAPE, SIZE, GROWTH RATE: Mounds of large leaves handsomely splashed or streaked with white or silver variegation. Flowers to 18 inches; foliage 15 inches tall and wide, spreading wider at a moderate pace.

ENVIRONMENTAL NOTES: Tolerates drought or heat but not at the same time.

USES: Coarse-mounded foliage anchors taller, arching plants such as Solomon's seal, columbine, great blue lobelia, bugbane, turtlehead, toad lily, or Jacob's ladder. Attracts hummingbirds.

CARE: Basically pest-free. Powdery mildew can develop. Bristly leaves are somewhat slug-resistant. No need to deadhead; flowering stalks are produced just once a year and lie down neatly as they age to be covered by the emerging large basal foliage. Self-sows and spreads by underground stolons to form weed-smothering colonies. Divide as desired in spring or fall. No need to cut the plants back in fall; foliage decomposes quickly over winter.

NOTES: 'Roy Davidson', a hybrid, has brilliant blue buds and flowers plus handsome, narrow, silver-spotted foliage. 'Milky Way' and 'Excalibur' were selected for even greater degrees of variegation. Zones 3–8.

'Sissinghurst White' lungwort has large white flowers and spotted leaves.

RANUNCULUS ACRIS

Swamp buttercup

18"

18"

- Full to half sun; tolerant of shade
- Any moist soil
- Average to wet
  - Deadhead after first bloom slows; branched flower stem
  - Rarely needs division; offsets
  - Staking unnecessary
  - Zones 3–8
  - Buttercup family

BLOOMS: Shining yellow flowers in airy masses from late spring to midsummer.

SHAPE, SIZE, GROWTH RATE: Mounded foliage to 18 inches tall and wide. Airy flowering stems to 3 feet. Clump. Fast growth rate.

ENVIRONMENTAL NOTES: Tolerant of salt, wide pH range, and wind. Not tolerant of heat and drought together.

USES: Filler between larger, later-emerging perennials in troublesome heavy soils and damp and wet areas. Combines well with Siberian iris, Joe-Pye weed, meadowsweet, queen-of-the-prairie, black-eyed Susan, swamp milkweed, tufted hair grass, and turtlehead.

CARE: Basically pest-free. Powdery mildew can occur where soil is dry. Deadhead after first flush of bloom slows by cutting back flower stalks to their base within the mounded basal foliage. Will repeat-bloom. Prolific self-sower. Cut to the ground in late fall or early spring. Rarely needs division; seedlings are always ready to replace any worn-out clumps.

NOTES: 'Flore Pleno', double-flowered variety. Lacks the airiness of the species as a filler plant.

'Flore Pleno' swamp buttercup

RODGERSIA AESCULIFOLIA

Fingerleaf rodgersia

2-4'

3-6'

- Half sun to shade
- Rich, even heavy soil with plentiful organic matter
- Constantly moist to soggy
- Deadheading not necessary
- Rarely needs division; hard to move
- Staking unnecessary
- Zones 5–8
- Saxifrage family

BLOOMS: Ivory flowers in dense clusters held high above the foliage; late spring.

SHAPE, SIZE, GROWTH RATE: Huge leaves in a mound 2 to 3 feet tall and up to twice as wide. Flower stalks rise to 4 feet. Clump. Slow growth rate.

ENVIRONMENTAL NOTES: Does not tolerate heat or full sun.

USES: Big, bold foliage makes most hostas look fine-textured in comparison. Acts as a focal point among other coarse-textured species. Plant with hosta, celandine poppy, snakeweed, and tovara. Also good with large, upright plants such as meadow rue, great Solomon's seal, cardinal flower, bugbane, and azure monkshood.

CARE: Basically pest-free. Deadheading not necessary; it will not stimulate additional bloom. Seed heads attractive and self-sowing is not a problem. Cut back in late fall or early spring. Enlist a friend when you decide to divide. Watch for wilting after moving.

NOTES: Flowers of featherleaf rodgersia (*R. pinnata*) are more spread out along its flowering stalk. 'Superba' foliage emerges bronze. Flowers pale pink. Zones 5–8.

Fingerleaf rodgersia (R. aesculifolia)

'Elegans' featherleaf rodgersia (R. pinnata) *has rose-pink blooms.*

RUDBECKIA FULGIDA 'GOLDSTURM'

Black-eyed Susan

30"

42"

- Full to half sun
- Any soil with plentiful organic matter
- Average to continuous moisture
- Deadhead to prolong bloom; branched flower stem
- Divide every four to five years to maintain vigor, size, and quantity of bloom; running; easy to move
- Staking unnecessary
- Zones 3–8
- Sunflower family

BLOOMS: Daisylike brassy-gold flowers with dark centers cover this large, mounded plant in mid- to late summer.

SHAPE, SIZE, GROWTH RATE: Dense mound of coarse, dark green foliage, 24 to 30 inches tall, 36 to 42 inches wide. Clump spreads by stolons and seed. Fast to very fast growth rate.

ENVIRONMENTAL NOTES: Tolerant of wet and poorly drained soil, wind, salt, and heat.

USES: Coarse texture and mounded shape combine well with finer textures and upright forms of ornamental grasses, ironweed, culver's root, speedwell, Joe-Pye weed, mugwort, false indigo, delphinium, crocosmia, globe thistle, and blazing star. Attracts birds and butterflies.

CARE: Basically pest-free. Leaf spot and crown rot may be present in older, crowded clumps. Leave the first sturdy seed stalks for winter interest. If birds do not eat all the seeds over winter, plants will self-sow to the point of being obnoxious. Cut back in late fall or, if leaving seed heads through winter, cut in early spring.

NOTES: 'Viette's Little Suzy' *R. fulgida speciosa* is a dwarf variety, 12 to 15 inches tall and wide.

Giant coneflower (*R. maxima*) has huge blue-green leaves and yellow flowers with prominent narrow cones, 4 to 8 feet tall and 2 to 3 feet wide. Just one of the many coneflower species worth considering for your perennial garden. Zones 5–9.

'Goldsturm' black-eyed Susan

SALVIA X SUPERBA

Perennial salvia

1½-2½'

1-2

- Full to half sun
- Well-drained soil
- Average moisture
- Deadhead as aging flower stalks begin to lean rather than stand straight; standard spike
- Divide every four to five years to rejuvenate clump; forked taproot
- Staking unnecessary

- Zones 4–8
- Mint family

BLOOMS: Densely packed violet or blue-violet flowers in narrow spikes. Late spring to early summer.

SHAPE, SIZE, GROWTH RATE: Short column, 15 to 30 inches tall depending on variety, 12 inches wide. Clump. Moderate to fast growth rate.

ENVIRONMENTAL NOTES: Tolerant of heat, drought, and wide pH range. Not tolerant of high humidity if hot.

USES: Shape helps blend small and large mounded plants: candytuft and pearly everlasting, dwarf aster and fountain grass, cranesbill and daylily, or catmint and peony. Spiky flowers contrast with rounded and flattened blooms: yarrow, globe flower, and coreopsis.

CARE: Basically pest-free; four-lined plant bug may disfigure leaves. Cut back just above main foliage mass. New flowering shoots develop near stem base. Self-sows. Forms a taproot that becomes increasingly resistant to division with time. Cut back in late fall or early spring.

'East Friesland' sports deep purple blooms and tolerates heat well; 18 inches tall.

'Purple Rain', Salvia verticillata

Mealy sage (Salvia farinacea) is an erect, 2- to 3-foot-tall plant with dark to silvery-blue blooms. Zones 7–9.

SAPONARIA OCYMOIDES

Soapwort

2-3"
18"

- Full to half sun
- Well-drained soil
- Average moisture
- Shear after bloom

- Divide in spring as desired; running; hard to move
- Staking unnecessary
- Zones 4–7
- Carnation family

BLOOMS: Rose-pink flowers cover this mat-forming plant in mid- to late spring.

SHAPE, SIZE, GROWTH RATE: A trailing mat that hugs the ground at 2 to 3 inches tall. Flowering stems sprawl 18 inches wide.

ENVIRONMENTAL NOTES: Does not tolerate wet or poorly drained soil or hot, humid summers.

USES: Combine with other perennials of winter interest such as sedum, coral bells, fountain grass, blue oat grass, lavender, 'Silver Mound' artemisia, rockcress, thrift, and big-root cranesbill. Attracts butterflies.

CARE: Basically pest-free. Shear after bloom to promote density, make the plant neater, and reduce self-sowing. Self-sown volunteers are almost always available to save you the trouble of division. Watch for wilting after moving.

NOTES: 'Rubra Compacta' is red-violet. Clumps are less wide-spreading than the species.

Soapwort

SCABIOSA CAUCASICA

Pincushion flower

2-2½' 1½'

- Full to half sun
- Well-drained sandy soil with plentiful organic matter
- Average to constant moisture
- Deadhead to prolong bloom; branched flower stems
- Divide every three to four years; offsets; easy to move
- Staking unnecessary
- Zones 3–8
- Teasel family

BLOOMS: The blue-violet, pink, or creamy white flowers look like wide lace trim around a pincushion. Early to midsummer.

SHAPE, SIZE, GROWTH RATE: Mostly basal foliage. Wiry, branched flower stalks to 30 inches long. Clump-forming. Moderate growth rate.

ENVIRONMENTAL NOTES: Tolerant of wind and a wide pH range. Does not tolerate high heat, high humidity, poor drainage, or wet soil but, the flowers are pretty enough to put out the effort to make plants happy.

USES: Flowers float far above their own insubstantial foliage, so combine them with plants of more substance. Plant in groups in front of or between 'Silver Brocade' artemisia, pearly everlasting, perennial bachelor's button, chrysanthemum, and Russian sage.

CARE: Basically pest-free. Four-lined plant bug may disfigure foliage. Rabbits may browse. Deadhead to prolong bloom, cutting first to side branches with flower buds, then removing the entire flowering stem. Self-sows. Seedling flower color varies.

Divide every three to four years to maintain good flowering and overall vigor.

NOTES: *S. columbaria* 'Butterfly Blue' and 'Pink Mist', 18 inches, flower from midsummer into fall if deadheaded. Plenty of flowers but without the willowy elegance of pincushion flower.

Pincushion flower

SEDUM SPECTABILE

Sedum

2-2½' 2½'

- Full sun
- Well-drained soil with plentiful organic matter
- Average moisture
- Do not deadhead
- Divide every four to five years; offsets
- Grow-through supports, if needed
- Zones 3–8
- Stonecrop family

BLOOMS: Flattened broccoli-like heads of pink, rose, or white in late summer.

SHAPE, SIZE, GROWTH RATE: Broad, coarse vase shape, 18 to 30 inches tall and wide. Clump. Fast growth rate.

ENVIRONMENTAL NOTES: Tolerates wind, heat, and high humidity but not wet soil or poor drainage.

USES: Good companion for salvia, yarrow, pincushion flower, ornamental mullein, golden marguerite, or bellflower.

CARE: Basically pest-free. Aphids and leaf spots can be a problem.

Staking not needed unless clumps are overcrowded or overfertilized. In late spring when temperatures reach 70° F, pinch stems to promote density, or place grow-through supports. Cut off old stems in early spring. Divide every four years or so for thick stems and heavy flowering.

NOTES: Hybrids: 'Autumn Joy' blooms later, has denser flower heads, and richer color in the seed heads. 'Vera Jameson', 12 inches or less, has blue-purple foliage and rose flowers in fall. 'Atropurpureum' has bronze-purple foliage and pink flowers.

'Rosy Glow' sedum is an 8-inch-tall hybrid sedum.

'Vera Jameson' sedum

'Autumn Joy' sedum

SIDALCEA MALVIFLORA
Checkerbloom

4'

2'

- Full to half sun
- Well-drained soil with plentiful organic matter
- Average to continuous moisture
- Deadhead for prolonged bloom and neater plant; multicluster
- Divide every three to four years; offsets
- Stake with grow-through supports, if necessary
- Zones 4–9
- Mallow family

BLOOMS: Spikes of 2-inch single hollyhock-shaped flowers in rose, pink, or white. Early summer.

SHAPE, SIZE, GROWTH RATE: A mound of foliage topped by tall, straight, unbranched stems. Overall, 2 to 4 feet tall, 1 to 2 feet wide. Clump. Moderate growth rate.

ENVIRONMENTAL NOTES: Does not tolerate drought or a combination of heat and humidity.

USES: Short vertical element to contrast with mat-forming plants such as lamb's-ears, soapwort, thyme, silver and wooly speedwells, Serbian bellflower, or pinks.

CARE: Basically pest-free but slugs and Japanese beetles may be a problem. Apply 50 percent more fertilizer than for average perennials. Clip stems to just above a large lower leaf when the stem has more spent blooms than flower buds. Divide every three to four years to renew the plant's vigor. Cut back in late fall or early spring.

NOTES: 'Party Girl', light pink flowers, 30 inches. 'Brilliant', deep rose, 30 inches.

Checkerbloom

STACHYS BYZANTINA
Lamb's-ears

½-1½'

1½'

- Full to half sun
- Well-drained, sandy soil
- Average moisture
- Deadhead; standard spike
- Divide every three to four years; running; easy to move
- Staking unnecessary
- Zones 4–7
- Mint family

BLOOMS: Tiny lilac-pink flowers obscured by gray flowering stems; early summer.

SHAPE, SIZE, GROWTH RATE: Forms a medium-textured gray mat 4 to 6 inches tall. Flowering stalks rise to 18 inches. Very fast growth rate.

ENVIRONMENTAL NOTES: Does not tolerate high heat and humidity, wet soil in winter, overly rich soil, or heavy fertilization.

USES: As edging for beds. Gray foliage contrasts with deep greens and blues of soapwort, thrift, myrtle spurge, sheep's fescue, and 'Vera Jameson' sedum.

CARE: Basically pest-free. Flea beetle may chew foliage. Fertilize at half the average perennial rate. Not grown for the flower, so deadhead as flowering stems appear, to keep new foliage coming at the base. Alternatively, grow a nonflowering or shy-flowering variety such as 'Silver Carpet' or 'Big Ears'. Divide every three to four years to restrict the spread and renew the soil beneath the original planting.

NOTES: Big betony (*S. macrantha*) forms a neat 8- to 12-inch mound of pebbly gray-green leaves with pink, white, or violet flowers on wiry stems 4 to 5 inches above the leaves. Better in heat and humidity than lamb's-ears. Zones 3–8.

Lamb's-ears

STOKESIA LAEVIS

Stokes' aster

8-18"

15"

- Full to half sun
- Well-drained, sandy soil with plentiful organic matter
- Average moisture
- Deadhead to prolong bloom; branched stems
- Divide every four to five years; offsets
- Staking unnecessary
- Zones 5–9
- Sunflower family

BLOOMS: Large blue-violet, white, or violet daisylike flowers with short, fine petals in mid- to late summer.
SHAPE, SIZE, GROWTH RATE: 18-inch-long flower stems over 8-inch-tall, 15-inch-wide basal foliage. Clump. Slow to moderate growth rate.
ENVIRONMENTAL NOTES: Does not tolerate drought.
USES: Coarse foliage and large flowers contrast with fine-textured thyme, artemisia, dropwort, candytuft, and lavender.
CARE: Basically pest-free. No need to cut back for winter; after deadheading, only the basal foliage remains. Divide to renew plant vigor.
NOTES: 'Blue Danube', blue. 'Omega Skyrocket', flowers white to lilac on stems double the normal height.

Stokes' aster

STYLOPHORUM DIPHYLLUM

Celandine poppy

18"

12"

- Half sun to shade
- Any soil with plentiful organic matter
- Average moisture
- Deadhead if desired; branched flower cluster
- Division not needed
- Staking unnecessary
- Zones 5–8
- Poppy family

BLOOMS: Gray-green foliage spangled with golden-orange flowers from mid- to late spring.
SHAPE, SIZE, GROWTH RATE: 18-inch-tall and 12-inch-wide clump. Moderate to fast growth.
ENVIRONMENTAL NOTES: Does not tolerate heat and sun.
USES: Brings gray and gold into the woodland garden. Pair it with yellow corydalis, gold-variegated hosta, purple-leaf coral bells, 'Brunette' fragrant bugbane, hakone grass, Jacob's ladder, columbine, or Serbian bellflower.
CARE: Basically pest-free. Deadhead if desired, although it's doubtful it extends the bloom season; volunteer seedlings are often welcome. No need to cut back in spring or fall; foliage decomposes quickly over winter.
NOTES: Often confused with the weedier greater celandine (*Chelidonium majus*), which spreads aggressively by seed.

Celandine poppy

TELLIMA GRANDIFLORA

Fringe cups

8"
21"

- Half sun to shade
- Well-drained soil with plentiful organic matter
- Average to continuous moisture

- Deadhead after bloom; standard spike
- Divide every four to five years; offsets
- Staking unnecessary
- Zones 5–8
- Rockfoil family

BLOOMS: Tiny fringed green cups on wiry, naked stems age to pinkish-green in midspring.

SHAPE, SIZE, GROWTH RATE: Mound of 8-inch-tall foliage, 21 inches wide, gradually increasing. Clump. Moderate growth rate.

ENVIRONMENTAL NOTES: Tolerates drought and competition from tree roots. Does not do well in combination of wet soil, high humidity, and heat, or with poor drainage.

USES: Dense-mounded evergreen foliage makes fine edging in the shade garden and a gray-green point of contrast among forest greens, bronzes, and blue-greens. Grow with blue-leaved hosta, columbine, meadow rue, fringed bleeding heart, dwarf goatsbeard, heart-leaf brunnera, dropwort, purple-leaf coral bells, bugbane, barrenwort, or astilbe.

CARE: Basically pest-free. Slug-resistant. Root weevils may be a problem. Deadhead after bloom to keep plant neat, unless self-sowing is important for naturalizing. Top-dress with 1 to 2 inches of compost every fall or very early spring. Divide every four to five years to maintain vigor and renew the soil. Mix compost into the soil when replanting.

NOTES: Flowers and flower stalks are more distinctly pink on 'Rubra' than the species.

Fringe cups

THALICTRUM ROCHEBRUNIANUM 'LAVENDER MIST'

Meadow rue

3-5'
2½'

- Full sun to shade
- Rich soil with plentiful organic matter

- Constantly moist to average to wet
- Not necessary to deadhead
- Divide after five to six years; running; hard to move
- May need staking; individual supports
- Zones 5–9
- Buttercup family

BLOOM TIME AND COLOR: Airy cloud of pale lavender flowers top the plant in midsummer.

SHAPE, SIZE, GROWTH RATE: Columnar, 3 to 5 feet tall and half as wide, medium to fine texture. Clump. Moderate growth rate.

ENVIRONMENTAL NOTES: The more sun, the more water the plant needs. Does not tolerate heat or drought. Grows poorly where summers are very hot and humid.

USES: In shade, grow it for its height; in moist sunny sites, grow it for fine texture. Plant with hostas, goatsbeard, astilbe, lungwort, rodgersia, and Japanese wax bell in the shade or Joe-Pye weed, hardy hibiscus, swamp milkweed, snakeweed and culver's root in wet sun.

CARE: Basically pest-free. Powdery mildew is sometimes seen when conditions are dry. Not necessary to deadhead; seed heads are almost as decorative as flowers. May need staking where light is strongly one-directional or soil is dry. Stake individual stems. Divide after five to six years to renew vigor; sooner if decline in height or bloom is noted. Cut back in late fall. Watch for wilting after moving.

NOTES: Tall meadow rue (*T. dasycarpum*) is more drought-tolerant. Blooms in late spring, 4 to 7 feet tall. Attractive with peony. Self-sows. New foliage may have purple highlights. Columbine meadow rue (*T. aquilegifolium*), 2 to 3 feet tall; in bloom, an upright baby's breath for the shade. Blooms in late spring. Zones 4–8. Yellow meadow rue (*T. delavayi*) has intense yellow-green flowers and seedpods, blue foliage. Beautiful with variegated blue-leaved hosta, 4 to 6 feet tall. Spreading rootstock. Requires staking. Zones 5–8.

'Lavender Mist'

THYMUS SERPYLLUM

Wild thyme

8"
24"

- Full sun
- Must have well-drained soil; prefers sandy soil where winters are wet
- Average moisture
- Shear after bloom
- Divide to renew vigor every three to four years; running; easy to move
- Staking unnecessary
- Zones 3–8
- Mint family

BLOOMS: From late spring to early summer, these fragrant evergreen mats are covered in tiny white, pale pink, or violet flowers.

SHAPE, SIZE, GROWTH RATE: Mat, 1 to 8 inches tall by 12 to 24 inches wide. Spreads by natural layering. Moderate to fast growth.

ENVIRONMENTAL NOTES: Tolerates half sun and shade of deciduous trees as well as light foot traffic, drought, wind, and heat.

USES: Grow as an edging with four-season interest; plant between larger perennials for better top-down viewing of plants with dark foliage. Combine with thrift or lamb's-ears. Plant under the skirts of vase-shaped, bare-ankle plants such as golden thyme, beneath butterfly weed and silver thyme, with sweet iris or wooly thyme, and around speedwell. Use around purple-leaf perennials such as coral bells, 'Vera Jameson' sedum, and purple sage.

CARE: Basically pest-free. Fertilize at half the average rate. Shear or mow after bloom to promote density. Divide to renew vigor every three to four years. Cut out sections, fill the void with compost and sand, then allow perimeter plants to recolonize the area. Do not cut this evergreen back hard in fall.

NOTES: Many varieties with silver or gold variegation and distinctive scents such as lemon and nutmeg.

Wild thyme

TIARELLA CORDIFOLIA

Allegheny foam flower

6"
12"

- Shade to half sun
- Well-drained soil with plentiful organic matter
- Average moisture
- Deadhead clump-forming types to prolong bloom; standard spike
- Divide every three to four years; offsets
- Staking unnecessary
- Zones 3–8
- Saxifrage family

BLOOMS: Tiny white to pale pink flowers clustered on short spikes in midspring.

SHAPE, SIZE, GROWTH RATE: Evergreen, 6-inch-tall mat. Spreads 12 inches or more by shallow underground or aboveground stolons. Moderate to fast growth.

ENVIRONMENTAL NOTES: Tolerates light foot traffic. Does not tolerate drought.

USES: Evergreen winter interest for shaded areas with coral bells, fringe cups, Lenten rose, Himalayan fleece flower, Serbian bellflower, barrenwort, dropwort, or candytuft.

CARE: Basically pest-free. Root weevils may be a problem. Divide every three to four years to reduce the spread if necessary. To maintain the vigor of clump-forming types, topdress with compost in late fall. Do not cut back in fall.

NOTES: Wherry's foam flower (*T. wherryi*) grows in clumps. It and hybrids of Allegheny foam flowers resemble coral bells in range of leaf size, coloration, and variegation: 'Dark Eyes', 'Tigerstripe', 'Iron Butterfly', and many other attractive varieties are available, with more being introduced every year.

'Spring Symphony' foam flower

POLYGONUM VIRGINIANUM 'PAINTER'S PALETTE'

Tovara

2'

2'

- Half sun to shade
- Any soil with plentiful organic matter
- Average to constant moisture
- Deadhead to prevent self-sowing; standard spike
- Divide every three to five years; running; easy to move
- Staking unnecessary
- Zones 4–8
- Buckwheat family

BLOOMS: Whiskerlike flower stalks; tiny, deep pink flowers top the stems in early to midsummer.

SHAPE, SIZE, GROWTH RATE: Upright arching to 2 feet tall and wide. Spreading by rhizomes. Growth rate varies with growing conditions, from slow in dry, lean soil to fast in moist, rich beds.

ENVIRONMENTAL NOTES: Drought-tolerant. Not tolerant of drying wind.

USES: Coarse, upright-arching profile provides contrast for mounded and fine-textured shade plants: small hostas, fringe cups, dwarf goatsbeard, astilbe, heart-leaf brunnera, fringed bleeding heart, yellow corydalis, cranesbill, and coral bells.

CARE: Basically pest-free. Foliage is the main show, not the flowers, so deadheading for continued bloom is not a priority. If plants begin to self-sow, as they sometimes can in rich, moist areas, deadheading may become more important. No need to cut plants down in fall or early spring; the stems and foliage decompose rapidly during winter. Divide every three to five years as necessary to restrict the spread.

NOTES: The variegated cultivars are much more attractive than the all-green species, which is nearly impossible to find. Foliage of 'Variegatum' has white markings; 'Painter's Palette' has white and rusty-pink ones.

'Variegatum' tovara

TRICYRTIS HIRTA

Toad lily

1½-3'

1½'

- Shade to half sun
- Moist, well-drained soil with plentiful organic matter
- Constant to average moisture
- Do not deadhead
- Divide every four to five years; offsets; easy to move
- Staking unnecessary
- Zones 4–9
- Lily family

BLOOMS: Creamy flowers with purple dots resemble orchids. Blooms are displayed on arching stems at each leaf axil in late summer to fall.

SHAPE, SIZE, GROWTH RATE: Upright arching shape; height varies with growing conditions. Moderate to fast growth rate.

ENVIRONMENTAL NOTES: Does not tolerate heat, drought, drying wind, or full sun. Plant in half sun rather than deep shade in colder zones to speed growth and ensure flowering before frost.

USES: Upright-arching shape and moderately coarse texture contrast with mounded shapes and fine textures in shaded areas: dwarf goatsbeard, barrenwort, hosta, astilbe, fringe cups, celandine poppy, heart-leaf brunnera, bleeding heart, woodland phlox, wild sweet william, and coral bells are good companions. Blooms with Japanese wax bell and latest-flowering Japanese anemones.

CARE: Basically pest-free. Rabbits and deer may sample the foliage. Leaf scorch is typical of plants stressed by heat, including reflected heat, and sun. No need to cut back in fall or early spring; stems and foliage decompose quickly over winter. Apply 50 percent more fertilizer than average.

Do not stake. Let stems arch outward as the season progresses to better display the flowers that are borne along the stems. Formosa toad lily bears its flowers at the tips of stems, so it can be staked without ruining the show. However, neither species will need staking if soil is rich and moist.

Divide every four to five years to restrict the spread and renew the plant's vigor. Mix compost into the soil before replanting.

NOTES: Formosa toad lily (*T. formosana*) blooms in mid- to late summer. Dark violet flowers on branched stalks from uppermost leaf axils. Deadhead to prolong bloom. Zones 5–9.

Toad lily

TROLLIUS X CULTORUM

Globe flower

18"

- Half sun to shade
- Rich soil with plentiful organic matter
18"
- Constantly moist to soggy
- Deadhead after bloom; branched flower stems
- Rarely needs division
- Staking unnecessary
- Zones 3–8
- Buttercup family

BLOOMS: Layered globes of lemon-yellow to orange petals, like big, fully double buttercups. Held on strong, nearly leafless stems high above the mounded basal foliage. Midspring.

SHAPE, SIZE, GROWTH RATE: Mounded, shiny foliage 12 to 18 inches tall and wide. Flower stalks make up the rest of the height. Clump. Moderate growth rate.

ENVIRONMENTAL NOTES: Tolerates a wide pH range and full sun and wind if soil is constantly moist and well-drained. Does not tolerate drought. Does poorly where the growing season is very hot.

USES: Yellow accents in spring. Plant with celandine poppy, fragrant bugbane, yellow corydalis, dropwort, hakone grass, and lungwort.

CARE: Basically pest-free. Powdery mildew can occur where soil is dry. Apply 50 percent more fertilizer than for average perennials. Deadhead after bloom for neat appearance.

NOTES: Orange globe flower (*T. ledebourii*) is later-blooming and taller, 3 to 4 feet tall. Midsummer. Zones 4–8.

Orange globe flower

VERBASCUM HYBRIDS

Ornamental mullein

1½-4'

- Full sun
- Well-drained, sandy soil
- Average to low moisture
2'
- Deadhead as seedpods begin to swell; standard spike
- Division not needed; root division; hard to move
- Staking unnecessary
- Zones 5–8
- Snapdragon family

BLOOMS: Cream, yellow or pink flowers on tall gray stalks. Early to midsummer.

SHAPE, SIZE, GROWTH RATE: Coarse mound of basal foliage 18 to 24 inches tall and wide. Flowering stems 3 to 4 feet tall. Clump. Fast growth.

ENVIRONMENTAL NOTES: Resistant to wind, drought, and heat. Does not tolerate high humidity, wet soil, or poor drainage.

USES: Vertical accent among mounded plants. Coarse gray foliage complements blue foliage and contrasts with finer textures: blue oat grass, sheep's fescue, fountain grass, myrtle spurge, cushion spurge, yarrow, dwarf aster, chrysanthemum, threadleaf coreopsis, perennial flax, and catmint. Attracts butterflies.

CARE: Basically pest-free. Fertilize at half the average rate. Deadhead as seedpods begin to swell at the base of the flowering stalk. Do not deadhead the last flowering stalk of the season. Because mulleins are short-lived, this provides self-sown replacements. Plants should not require staking. If stems lodge, cut back on fertilizer or move where plants will get more sun. Watch for toppling after moving. Do not divide. To propagate identical plants, take root cuttings in second spring. Remove last flower stalk once seed has ripened, but do not cut down basal foliage in fall.

NOTES: 'Cotswold' hybrids offer a good range of colors.

'Gainsborough' grows 3 to 4 feet tall and has pale yellow blooms.

VERNONIA NOVEBORACENSIS

New York Ironweed

3-7'

1-2'

- Full to half sun
- Well-drained soil with plentiful organic matter
- Average moisture
- Deadheading not necessary
- Divide after seven to eight years; offsets; easy to move
- Stake tall types; grow-through support or individual braces
- Zones 4–9
- Aster family

BLOOMS: Dark purple and red-violet flowers in large, flat-topped clusters in mid- to late summer.

SHAPE, SIZE, GROWTH RATE: Upright column or vase shape, 3 to 7 feet tall and 1 to 2 feet wide. Moderate growth rate.

ENVIRONMENTAL NOTES: Resistant to wind, drought, heat, and humidity. Does not tolerate wet or poorly drained soil.

USES: Tall accent plant and coarse, dark green foliage complements ornamental grasses, many-flowered sunflower, purple bush clover, culver's root, black-eyed Susan, patrinia, mugwort, queen-of-the-prairie, peony, and hardy hibiscus. Attracts butterflies.

CARE: Basically pest-free. Tallest types may require staking. Stems can be pinched several times between spring and early summer to promote density and reduce height. Long-lived. Divide after seven to eight years to maintain vigor and free flowering. Cut back in late fall or early spring.

NOTES: There are many ironweed species ranging widely in height, color, and size of flowers and leaves. Most plants currently on the market are hybrids of uncertain parentage. Ironweed is relatively new to gardens; watch for growers to begin to sort out and name the many selections. All the species have garden value, so grow any variety you find.

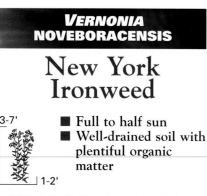

New York ironweed

VERONICA LONGIFOLIA

Long-leaf veronica

2-3'

1½'

- Full to half sun
- Well-drained soil with plentiful organic matter
- Average moisture
- Deadhead to prolong bloom; standard spike
- Divide every four to five years; offsets
- Grow-through supports or crutches, if needed
- Zones 4–8
- Snapdragon family

BLOOMS: Blues, violets, pinks, and whites from mid- to late summer.

SHAPE, SIZE, GROWTH RATE: Columnar, 2- to 3-foot-tall clump. Moderate growth rate.

ENVIRONMENTAL NOTES: Wind-resistant. Does not tolerate drought, wet soil, or high humidity.

USES: Vertical accent with catmint, mums, fountain grass, bloody cranesbill, and black-eyed Susan. Dark green foliage complements artemisia, tufted hair grass, and thyme. Spike flowers contrast with round blooms

CARE: Leaf spot and mildew can be problems. Cut back in late fall or early spring. Divide to maintain vigor and free flowering.

NOTES: 'Sunny Border Blue' is a long-blooming, dark blue hybrid. 'Blue Pyramid' has medium blue flowers in midsummer, 24 inches tall. Alpine speedwell (*V. alpina*) is a mat-forming, spring-blooming miniature less than 12 inches tall.

Long-leaf veronica

Spike speedwell (V. *spicata*) *blooms in early to midsummer in blue, pink or white.*

Woolly speedwell (V. *incana*) *is a spreading plant with dark blue flower spikes in mid- to late spring.*

VERONICASTRUM VIRGINICUM

Culver's root

4-6'

1-2'

- ■ Half to full sun
- ■ Moist soil with plentiful organic matter
- ■ Constantly moist to average
- ■ Deadhead to prolong bloom
- ■ Division not needed; offsets; easy to move
- ■ May require staking; crutches or grow-through support
- ■ Zones 4–8
- ■ Snapdragon family

BLOOMS: White to pale pink spires in midsummer.

SHAPE, SIZE, GROWTH RATE: 4- to 6-foot-tall and 2-foot-wide clumps. Moderate growth rate.

ENVIRONMENTAL NOTES: Tolerates wet soil. Not tolerant of heat.

USES: Vertical accent with mounded hardy hibiscus, perennial ageratum, and perennial bachelor's button. Spike flowers contrast with many-flowered sunflower, black-eyed Susan, yarrow, and Joe-Pye weed. Architectural foliage adds interest to ornamental grasses.

CARE: Basically pest-free. May require staking in average to dry soil. Use crutches or grow-through supports. Deadhead to prolong bloom. Cut back in late fall or early spring. May provide winter interest if well-grown; otherwise, seed heads will shatter.

NOTES: 'Roseum' flowers have pink flush.

Culver's root

Veronicastrum virginicum *var.* incarnatum

INDEX

Note: Page numbers in **boldface type** indicate Plant Gallery references; page numbers in ***bold italic type*** indicate photographs or illustrations.

USDA PLANT HARDINESS ZONE MAP

This map of climate zones helps you select plants for your garden that will survive a typical winter in your region. The United States Department of Agriculture (USDA) developed the map, basing the zones on the lowest recorded temperatures across North America. Zone 1 is the coldest area and Zone 11 is the warmest.

Plants are classified by the coldest temperature and zone they can endure. For example, plants hardy to Zone 6 survive where winter temperatures drop to –10° F. Those hardy to Zone 8 die long before it's that cold. These plants may grow in colder regions but must be replaced each year. Plants rated for a range of hardiness zones can usually survive winter in the coldest region as well as tolerate the summer heat of the warmest one.

To find your hardiness zone, note the approximate location of your community on the map, then match the color band marking that area to the key.

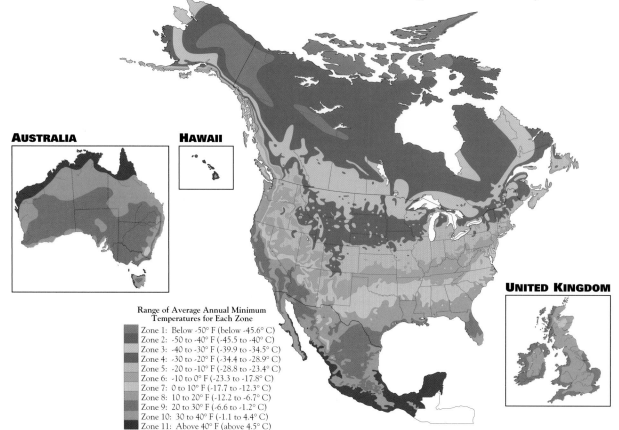

AUSTRALIA

HAWAII

UNITED KINGDOM

Range of Average Annual Minimum Temperatures for Each Zone

Zone 1: Below -50° F (below -45.6° C)
Zone 2: -50 to -40° F (-45.5 to -40° C)
Zone 3: -40 to -30° F (-39.9 to -34.5° C)
Zone 4: -30 to -20° F (-34.4 to -28.9° C)
Zone 5: -20 to -10° F (-28.8 to -23.4° C)
Zone 6: -10 to 0° F (-23.3 to -17.8° C)
Zone 7: 0 to 10° F (-17.7 to -12.3° C)
Zone 8: 10 to 20° F (-12.2 to -6.7° C)
Zone 9: 20 to 30° F (-6.6 to -1.2° C)
Zone 10: 30 to 40° F (-1.1 to 4.4° C)
Zone 11: Above 40° F (above 4.5° C)

METRIC CONVERSIONS

U.S. Units to Metric Equivalents			Metric Units to U.S. Equivalents		
To Convert From	Multiply By	To Get	To Convert From	Multiply By	To Get
Inches	25.4	Millimeters	Millimeters	0.0394	Inches
Inches	2.54	Centimeters	Centimeters	0.3937	Inches
Feet	30.48	Centimeters	Centimeters	0.0328	Feet
Feet	0.3048	Meters	Meters	3.2808	Feet
Yards	0.9144	Meters	Meters	1.0936	Yards

To convert from degrees Fahrenheit (F) to degrees Celsius (C), first subtract 32, then multiply by 5/9.

To convert from degrees Celsius to degrees Fahrenheit, multiply by 9/5, then add 32.